Sword

of

Submission

Reclaiming the power of being human

By

Jody Mayhew & Dan Mayhew

two worlds press

Dedication

To the late Dr. Joseph C. Aldrich whose call to prayer has brought unity to the church, and who valued Jody and her ministry. Without his encouragement, this book would not have been written.

Contents

A study/discussion guide (PDF) is available for download at
www.stonebutterfly.net

Preface

There is a hermeneutical principle that goes something like, "where the Bible is explicit we are bound; where the Bible is ambiguous or silent we are free insofar as the exercise of our freedom does not violate any established biblical principle." It is an argument for the consistent application of Scripture, and a good one. Building doctrinal and theological foundations on silence or ambiguity is a recipe for confusion and, at worst, heresy. Coherent faith has to be based on clearly stated propositions, not on presumption. Case closed.

But…

Is clearly articulated doctrine and systematic theology the sum of Christian faith? At the risk of causing biblical purists some anxiety, let me suggest that reducing Christian faith to doctrine and proposition has drained Christianity of its immediacy and its narrative consistency. Often, after we have parsed our faith and assigned to its component parts all the relevant explicit doctrinal passages, we end up handing new believers an outlined list of theological proofs: whoever believes in Him will have eternal life; the just will live by faith; I will come again; all scripture is useful; behold I stand at the door; take my yoke; by grace you have been saved…

We build our faith on the bedrock of orthodoxy. Unfortunately, the picture of what we believe often doesn't fit together. One Sunday school student amazed his parents by describing how "Solomon had skewered the Philippines with the jawbone of an ass." Kids wonder about the baby Jesus and "round John Virgin"; about apostles, epistles, and disciples; about Noah and the ark, Moses and the ark, Joan of Arc. Most

i

adult Christians are not that bewildered, but even they may have all the foundational information without knowing where it fits. Many people who as children learn about the Bible never gain a sense of the whole. They know those explicit verses about Jesus being the Son of God who died for the sins of the world; and about salvation by grace and the need to accept Jesus by faith, but many do not have much sense of how it all fits together. In short, adult Christians can share their faith as a list of doctrinal imperatives—a volume of revised statutes—but can't express their faith in a way that most non-believers can absorb, in narrative form.

These days, propositions and doctrinal statements aren't enough. Not even close. Postmodern thinking yearns for the whole story, the panorama, and the meta-narrative. Postmoderns have questions that often don't have as much to do with information as they do with application. What is the big picture? Does your list of doctrinal imperatives and propositional truths work? And if so, for whom? Where does all this fit? And, most importantly, what is my place in the story now?

Sword of Submission is not an attempt to build theology. Doctrine and theology are best drawn from those explicit passages, as in fact, they have been. But what about the back-story, the plot? How does it all work out in real time? For that, we would argue, we can safely turn to those ambiguous passages and to those places where the Bible is tellingly silent. From these we may be able to draw the narrative, the vast sweep of the greatest story ever told and find our place in it.

Acknowledgements

These thoughts would not have become a book without having been tried out on numerous people who listened patiently, responded encouragingly, objected respectfully and, in the end, agreed that what they had heard changed them for the better. We thank the "young marrieds" of Montavilla Baptist Church for sharing this journey and for patiently waiting for us to put our classroom discussions into print. Also, thanks to John Barnhill, who helped organize the first drafts so many years ago; Anna Seley for her careful read-through and to Adam Shields, Rob Robinson, Julie Tadema, Ron Mar, Suzie Ford and Steve Price for being willing to offer thoughts on the project. And to Melodie Steele for wielding her fine-toothed comb so skillfully.

Prologue:

A Reunion with Angels

Call it instinct. Or natural knowledge. Call it a primal hunch. Whatever it is, it shows up all over in legend and literature, in the stories we tell, even in the movies we fork out ten bucks to go see. Throughout the narrative tradition of the human race there are references to worlds unseen, known only in part, tantalizingly close yet just out of reach. There are tales of unknown beings and unnatural powers.

Why are those references so pervasive? Are we humans just imaginative creatures that happen to return to the same themes over and over? Or does that give us too much credit? Maybe what we call fantasy really descends from what could be called the "meta-narrative" of the universe. Elves and angels; orcs and demons. The rebellion of Star Wars—may the Force be with you. The interface of worlds in The Matrix. Our imagination? Human creativity? Or is there a suggestion woven into the soul of the human race, a yearning to know of things invisible—a longing to be somehow whole again. Maybe that's why we write about it and imagine it. We call it fantasy. On the other hand, it could be evidence that our souls are like restless fish, aching to return to the very headwaters of creation. What might we find there?

We think we will find that our stories come from an instinctive connection with the Bible and its story. Consider a letter written in the first century:

You have not come to a physical mountain, to a place of flaming fire, darkness, gloom, and whirlwind… No, you have come to … the city of the living God, the heavenly Jerusalem, and to thousands of angels in joyful assembly. You have come to the assembly of God's firstborn children, whose names are written in heaven. You have come to God himself, who is the judge of all people. And you have come to the spirits of the redeemed in heaven who have now been made perfect. You have come to Jesus, the one who mediates the new covenant between God and people…

~The Letter to the Hebrews (NLT)

Try to imagine what the writer to the Hebrews is describing here. Imagine this "heavenly city." It is not only a gathering place for angels, but a welcome hang-out for human beings— eternal beings and "time-creatures" meeting together in one place! The race of eternal ones is having a joyous celebration, a party. Imagine that! Thousands from the race of angels cheering and shouting! Why the celebration? Perhaps it is because of the time creatures—humans—the church of the firstborn. Is it a victory celebration? A welcoming party? A reception? Perhaps it is all of those things and one more. Perhaps a reunion.

I think the writer to the Hebrews is drawing on some common understanding of the meta-narrative of creation; that the universe is bi-dimensional, each one with its native race; that there has existed a chasm between the two that will one day be bridged and the way opened for a gathering of races. Not a first encounter but a return to the way things were always meant to be, a reunion. In the book of Hebrews, God is foreshadowing for us the celebration when those two dimensions come together, humans and angels by the grace of God in Christ celebrating the victory over a rebellion that broke out in eternity. The party is the sign that the rebellion has been put down and the army of rebel angels destroyed. It is the symbol of the rescue of the human race, nearly doomed in the fierce battle over creation.

The Bible is a war story. It tells of the liberation of creation by a hero first called The Seed who faced death and the fury of a rebel army of eternal beings. It is the tale of a conflict, the outcome of which hangs on a race of "time creatures" and their willingness to become allies with The Seed and submit themselves to their Creator. Fantasy? We don't think so. Perhaps some fantasies are merely reality viewed through a one-dimensional lens. Perhaps the human race—beings stranded in time, "time-creatures"—really are part of an invisible war that broke out in another dimension and is, even now, being fought across the battlefield of time and space. Perhaps the prize is a seamless creation, a multi-dimensional universe no longer divided, but brought back together—everything in the eternal dimension and in time/space submitted under the authority of The Seed. The biblical story of redemption is the story of the defeat of a rebel army in the eternal realm, and of the liberation of a race once captive in time and space. In the end, it is the story of a joyous army that wins the war by using the most sophisticated weapon available—and it's been available for a very long time.

PART 1

Battle Lines

Chapter 1

The Shape of the Universe

In the beginning God created the heavens and the earth...

So where was God before that? I can tell you where he *wasn't*. He was not in heaven.

According to bumper sticker theologians, the matter of beginnings, sometimes called "the big bang," is settled: "God said it and, Bang! The universe!" Cute. But, if we're not careful we will run right past the beginning without giving any thought to what came before. That there was a beginning is only part of the story in the first five words of the Bible.

It comes clearer if we stop at the fourth word: In the beginning, *God...* More than just establishing that creation had a beginning, the first four words establish what was there at the start—even before the beginning.

It was God. Period. An infinite, eternal, conscious personality. God and nothing else.

God was there and then he made the universe. We sometimes envision God being in heaven, when in fact, he existed before heaven. He didn't have to make a place for himself *to be*, he already *was*. He was around before he made anything. The ancient writings say, "Far below him are the heavens and the earth. He stoops to look…" [1] We would like to be able to understand this, but I am afraid we're sitting on the wrong side of eternity. The best we can do is rely on the Hebrew poet when he says God is "enthroned on high." Where that is we don't know, but logically, at least in Genesis 1 it wasn't in heaven.

In the Bible the word, heaven gets translated several different ways.[2] One refers to the sky closest to us where the birds fly and snowballs are thrown. Wind blows through this heaven, and clouds. We could call this, "the first heaven" or "heaven #1." So, is there a second heaven? Some scholars suggest that the King James word "firmament" may describe the sky that is out of our reach where hang the sun, moon and stars (higher than you can throw a snowball). They suggest that this could amount to a "second heaven" in the ancient writer's thinking. That would explain the Apostle Paul talking about being caught up to a "third heaven" in his letter to the church in Corinth.[3] It is clear from his writing that he expects the Corinthians to understand that being in the "third heaven" meant he had seen into an eternal realm and not the world we live in, namely the sense-world with sights, sounds, smells and touch. When Paul spoke of the third heaven he was talking about *another dimension.* In the Old Testament the term "highest heaven" is used to describe that same thing.[4]

This brings us back to Genesis 1. God created "the heavens" and "the earth." The latter, earth, is a dimension of time and space. But at least one of the former, one of the

---

[1] Psalm 113:6 (NLT).
[2] The Hebrew word for "heavens; heaven; sky" transliterated "shamayim" is a general Semitic word that appears in languages such as Ugaritic, Akkadian, Aramaic, and Arabic. It occurs 420 times and in all periods of biblical Hebrew and is used as many as five different ways depending on context (from *Vine's Expository Dictionary of Biblical Words* ©1985, Thomas Nelson Publishers).
[3] 2 Corinthians 12:2.
[4] 1 Kings 8:27.

heavens, is something different. That means the universe is made in at least two dimensions: one wrapped up in time, and the other infinite and eternal. This is consistent with all those tales of unseen worlds and the supernatural. It is also very important because the whole narrative of Judeo-Christian thought hinges on this reality. If we get tangled up in the hands of the clock and burdened by the weight of the tangible world we will miss the destiny of creation. Paul, in a different letter written to the Christ-followers in the city of Ephesus, explained what God intended for his creation. He put it this way—the important part is in italics: "At the right time he will bring everything together under the authority of Christ—*everything in heaven and on earth.*"[5]

Here both dimensions are mentioned. God's plan is to somehow bring them together. That shouldn't be a big surprise; after all, the Bible frequently speaks of God's authority in heaven and earth making it clear that he has a stake in both. Even so, we don't think about heaven very often except as an ultimate destination, as though it will be important one day, but right now it isn't of much use. I guess we shouldn't be too hard on ourselves about that. Unlike Paul, we haven't had much experience with that other dimension. Still, if God intends to bring everything in heaven and earth together, then the eternal dimension must be relevant to us—and not just in some far off future.

Here's why: we are not alone—as a race, I mean. Jump ahead in Genesis to the second chapter and that becomes clear. I've been using the New Living Translation, but here I'll use the New American Standard, not just because it's my favorite, but also because it captures the meaning of the verse better. Here's what it says: "Thus the heavens and the earth were completed, *and all their hosts.*"[6] I have italicized the last part because it tells us something very important. The word "hosts" usually means people or armies so the verse says that there are

---

[5] Ephesians 1:10.
[6] Genesis 2:1.

not just people on earth, but also people in heaven, not time-and-space people like us, but created beings nonetheless, each with a mind, will, even emotions. There, in the eternal dimension, is a race of "eternal ones." From our perspective we call them "supernatural beings." The Bible calls them angels, holy ones, mighty ones, morning stars, elohim, and sons of God. They live, as it were, in a parallel universe.

It probably needs to be said that there are some who aren't convinced that the word "hosts" is talking about angels. They suggest that it could be referring to a host of stars and observable heavenly phenomena. I suppose that could be, but in context it is hard to imagine that in heaven we have stars—the word literally means "armies" remember—and only on earth do we have people. That is unless the whole subject of angels just makes us nervous, which would be what's called an *a priori* assumption: letting our biases determine our conclusions. Such a conclusion seems unnecessary when you consider how many times the Bible mentions heaven having inhabitants or uses stars as an analogy for angels.

Consider Psalm 29:1. "Give honor to the Lord, you angels; give honor to the Lord for his glory and strength." Or Psalm 89:7 where it says, "The highest angelic powers stand in awe of God. He is far more awesome than those who stand around his throne." There are other passages, too, but the bottom line is that there are eternal beings in the eternal dimension. Creatures who are indigenous to eternity, with peculiar qualities suited to that environment.

Now, here's the question: So what? Do they have anything to do with us? I wouldn't be surprised.

Snake in the Grass

The creation story in Genesis seems like familiar ground, but there are a few things that are often passed over, particularly when we note that the narrative is only told from the perspective of one dimension—there are two, remember.

Let's zoom in on some parts of the story. Start with Genesis 1:26.

> Then God said, "Let us make people in our image, to be like ourselves. They will be masters over all life—the fish in the sea, the birds in the sky, and all the livestock, wild animals, and small animals." So God created people in his own image; God patterned them after himself; male and female he created them. God blessed them and told them, "Multiply and fill the earth and subdue it. Be masters over the fish and birds and all the animals." And God said, "Look! I have given you the seed-bearing plants throughout the earth and all the fruit trees for your food.

A couple of notes before we dig in. First, notice that God refers to himself as "we." The learned ones of the Bible have different thoughts on why he does this. Some see it as what is called a "royal we" which may have been part of the way that the biblical writers assigned honor to kings or, in this case, to God. Other scholars point out that the word for God in the original language is a plural so the translation needs to be plural. Finally, some speculate that God is, by nature, three persons (that's where the term "trinity" comes in). That makes God "a community of one." One thing on which reputable scholars agree is that God is not one of a bunch of gods. He isn't talking to his fellow gods. The Bible makes that pretty clear when it says, "Hear, O Israel! The LORD is our God, the LORD is one!"[7] God, the one God that existed before the two dimensions were made, is the only one of his kind, but because he is present in all the dimensions simultaneously he is also more than one. He existed before there were dimensions, which makes him—work with me here—"bigger" than the things he made. He can be "in" each of the dimensions, but not completely because he is more than they can hold without bursting the seams. In the New Testament book of Colossians Paul writes, "For in Christ the fullness of God lives in a human

---

[7] Deuteronomy 6:4.

body…" Jesus was the time/space package that God used in order to be present in our dimension. As much of God as could be contained within the limitations of time and space was there in the man we call Jesus Christ, who was called in ancient times, "The Seed."[8]

Secondly, God speaks of making people in his own image. I have more to say about this later, but for now let me assure you that the Bible isn't saying that we look like God in a physical sense. There are other ways that we are similar to him that are more important.

Thirdly, God gives the time-creatures something to do. He gives them the job of having children and making other people like themselves and, in the process, going out into the world to fill it.

Finally, God gives humans the responsibility of being master over the animals. The creature, Adam, is given the privilege of actually naming them. Furthermore, the passage suggests that they were all, humans included, herbivores at that time. They were plant eaters. You can conclude that if nobody was prowling around the garden intending to make a meal out of anybody else, things were pretty peaceful and harmonious. My point, though, is that the responsibility people had over the animals puts them all squarely in the dimension of time and space. They are indigenous to the temporal dimension.

But are they confined there? In the next few verses Genesis reveals an interesting fact: somewhere in the garden there is a connection to the eternal dimension. It is referred to as "the tree of life" and there is reason to believe that, whatever it was (or they were. Perhaps it was a species as opposed to a particular tree) its fruit was free for the taking and we find out at the end of Genesis 3 that the implication was that if the time-creatures did eat from that tree they would live forever! As far as we can understand from our vantage point in time and space, living forever isn't for us, but was it always that

---

[8] Genesis 3:15 (KJV).

way? Perhaps we were designed to be "spiritual amphibians"[9] native to one dimension but free and comfortable to be a part of another. The presence of that tree makes you wonder.

But what about the other race, the one native to eternity? Did they have similar ability? Were they "amphibians," too? The answer is, yes.

In the third chapter of Genesis another character shows up. He is called "serpent" and the Bible says he is one crafty customer.

> Now the serpent was the shrewdest of all the creatures the LORD God had made. "Really?" he asked the woman. "Did God really say you must not eat any of the fruit in the garden?"

> "Of course we may eat it," the woman told him. "It's only the fruit from the tree at the center of the garden that we are not allowed to eat. God says we must not eat it or even touch it, or we will die."

> "You won't die!" the serpent hissed. "God knows that your eyes will be opened when you eat it. You will become just like God, knowing everything, both good and evil."[10]

There are some questions that need answering. Who is this serpent? What did he look like? How did he get into the garden? And finally, what's he up to?

Until now, in the time/space dimension there are only two intelligent creatures that are capable of having a reasoned conversation, Adam and Eve. Yet, here is this being called

---

[9] An amphibian is an animal that can function comfortably on water and on land. Spiritual amphibians would be creatures that could function in more than one dimension. Obedient angels do this numerous times throughout the Bible—they visit planet earth "on official business" about 30 times. It is possible that even the disobedient ones did for a while for nefarious purposes. We are suggesting that humans may have been originally designed with similar ability.

[10] Genesis 3:1-5 (NLT).

"the serpent" hanging out in the garden, in the midst of it, actually. The New Living Translation embellishes the dialogue with some snaky qualities, he "hisses." But hold on a minute. This isn't your garden-variety snake. I've never known a snake to say anything intelligent or even act as though it was interested in conversation. This one is different. Indeed, there is a positive identification of this being in the last book of the Bible, the book of Revelation. In Revelation 12:9 the serpent is identified as Satan, the Devil.

And who, or more appropriately, *what* might he be? Here's what the scholars think: he is one of those eternal ones. He is one of the "hosts" mentioned in Genesis 2, a being created for the eternal dimension. Powerful and, Genesis says, more subtle and shrewd, than any other creature—certainly than any of the animals—in time or eternity. He was outright sneaky and a bald-faced liar. Notice how deftly he steered the conversation toward the one thing in all the Garden of Eden that the Creator had forbidden people to eat, and then how he accuses God of having hidden motives because of it. Clearly, the serpent is not on God's side.

Not only that, the Bible holds evidence that the eternal ones were already in the heavenly places before the time of the Garden of Eden. Let's briefly visit the book of Job in the Bible. We'll be revisiting this interesting book later, but for now, let's look at Job 38, verses four through seven. Here God is talking to Job, who as you may recall, was a good man that had come upon what appeared to be some incredibly bad luck: financial setbacks, multiple deaths in the family, and health totally gone to pot. To make matters worse, he had some friends who came over to visit him in his misfortune who were a real pain. Eventually, Job just loses it and starts to complain about God, the universe and his circumstances in general. That's when God loses patience and has a few things of his own to say to Job. As he does, we learn something about the order of the universe. Listen:

Where were you when I laid the foundations of the earth? Tell me, if you know so much. Do you know how its dimensions were determined and who did the surveying? What supports its foundations, and who laid its cornerstone as the morning stars sang together and all the angels shouted for joy? [11]

Did you catch that? Who was there singing and shouting? Eternal beings. Morning stars (that's a Bible code phrase for eternal beings) and angels—already there before the Creator was finished creating! Later (we don't know how much later since time hadn't been invented yet) some of these same beings splinter off and form a rebel army. It is apparently the rebel chief that turns up in time and space talking smack about the Creator.

So, what else do we know about this "serpent?" Well, for one thing, he wasn't a snake. Most of the time when artists try to picture this encounter with Eve (and Adam, by the way. Evidently, he was standing right there. Look at Genesis 3:6.) there is a snake, forked tongue and all, curled around an apple tree having a conversation with Eve. Is that how it happened?

First of all, I can't imagine anybody feeling attracted to a big snake. I'd be keeping my distance. Of course, since the first people lived in a completely safe and harmonious environment we can let that pass. In those days they may have thought a snake was cute. Still, I should think that a talking snake would have been unusual to Adam and Eve. If it was, nothing is mentioned. But later, we find a clue that the serpent may not have been a snake at that first meeting.

I don't think I'm being a spoiler by telling you that later in the story, after Adam and Eve cave in to the serpent's deception, God comes looking for them. According to Genesis, God appears in the garden and calls out to his time-creatures who—get this—are hiding in the bushes from the all-knowing God. That they were hiding indicates that something about their assessment of God has changed. He has gotten smaller to them somehow. That God plays along and asks them where

---

[11] Job 38:4.

they are should remind us of something: when God asks a question it isn't because he needs information, it's because *you* need information. The answer to God's question always tells you something about yourself.

So here is the Creator standing in the time/space dimension. And here are three creatures, an eternal being and two time-creatures, who have been caught red-handed stepping out of harmony with the plan of the One who created everything, having joined themselves together in a rebellion. Now, the Creator explains the consequences of this act of "tree-sin." I'll return to the consequences that Adam and Eve faced in the next chapter but, for now, I want to call your attention to the consequence God aims at the serpent in verse 14:

> Because you have done this, you will be punished. You are singled out from all the domestic and wild animals of the whole earth to be cursed. You will grovel in the dust as long as you live, crawling along on your belly.

Notice that last phrase? "Crawling along on your belly." That God has placed this curse on the serpent begs the question, if this creature is going to crawl from now on, how did he get around before? Did he have legs on a long snaky body? Did he roll around lengthwise like a pole? Or hop on his tail like an organic pogo stick? Or was he something else entirely? I suggest that he appeared as so many other angelic beings in the Bible appear, like a man, attractive and persuasive. Here was an eternal being disguised in flesh, intending to make spiritual slaves of the race of time-creatures. In response, God intervenes and pronounces a curse that is to become a sign for all the generations of humans: the sign of the serpent, a reminder of this deception and its perpetrator. From this day forward, the leader of the rebellion in the eternals will be known as "the serpent" among the creatures of the temporal dimension.

So, how did the being we have come to know as "the serpent" get into this dimension? The easy answer is that God let him in, and I suppose that's true, but why? How?

One possibility is that this was all God's idea. Imagine the phone ringing in Lucifer's apartment. (Lucifer is the name often assigned to Satan). It's God's appointment secretary telling him that God wants to see him right away. Lucifer goes. God tells him that he has made the Garden of Eden and that he has put one no-no in it and he is going to send Lucifer to see if he can seduce the people in the garden to be disobedient. Sort of a test.

Sorry, but that just doesn't seem like a logical way for the serpent to get into the garden. That God was an accomplice in some deliberate plan to bring humans to a fallen state doesn't ring true. I don't mean to imply that God is anything but sovereign and all-powerful, as though he made the universe and let it get out of control, but that the serpent, and the deception of humans, and the pollution of the temporal dimension was God's first choice seems like a stretch to me. It makes more sense that these creatures acted defiantly and independently.

Indeed, there are places in the Bible where what God wants and what his creation does are two very different things. For example, when the Israelites wandered in the wilderness God provided food for them. It was called, "manna."[12] Eventually, the people got tired of eating the same thing day after day and whined about it so much God sent quail into the camp—lots of quail. They were nearly buried in them. Later, in the Psalms, we learn that their whining may have gotten them a change in diet, but they suffered from spiritual malnutrition that came when God yielded his first choice and gave them what they wanted. In another place the Israelites get the idea they want to have a king. God lets them have one, but not before making it clear that having a king was not his first choice for them.[13] Predictably there are negative repercussions.

---

[12] You can find the story of the Israelites' complaint and a description of 'manna,' that miracle food, in Numbers 11. Further reference to it is made in Exodus 16 and elsewhere.

[13] The story is found in 1 Samuel 8.

I think the serpent in the Garden of Eden was like that. Humans can reject God's first choice and do as they please; likewise eternal beings. This was an act of disobedience on Lucifer's part that had dire consequences in time and space. How did the serpent get into the garden? He decided to go. As a "spiritual amphibian" he could enter time and space. There are accounts all through the Bible of the eternal ones doing just that. Their ability to cross the border between the dimensions isn't in question biblically. And apparently, neither is their freedom to do so. Clearly, the serpent isn't in the garden on a mission from God. He is a rebel from the eternal dimension. Furthermore, there are other rebels in that dimension, an army of them. In the book of Revelation we are told there was warfare in the eternal dimension and that a rebel army was defeated there.[14] This isn't the stuff of fantasy. On the contrary, what we regard as fantasy may be the stuff of history. As a race, we may give ourselves too much credit for imagination. Tolkien's orc armies and battling races may not be creative invention, but part of a collective memory drawn from that "meta-narrative" of creation. We call encounters with an unseen realm myth and legend. I suggest that myth and legend are more than they appear.

Finally, what is this eternal con-artist up to? It is plain that he has an agenda. It's unlikely that it was mere coincidence that he dropped in on the first couple just as they happened to be strolling past the tree of the knowledge of good and evil, the one tree in the garden that God had forbidden them to have anything to do with. Furthermore, as long as we're talking about this tree, what were Adam and Eve even doing near it, anyway? Hadn't God instructed them to go out into the world? "Multiply and fill the earth and subdue it…" is the way he put it. So what are they doing near that tree *in the center of the garden* when they should have been making plans to go out and fill the earth? This is a setup. My hunch is that if they had

---

[14] The story is in the last book of the Bible, *Revelation*, in the twelfth chapter.

been paying attention to what the Creator had told them to do we wouldn't be having the problems we're having in the world today—but I digress. Or maybe I don't. Maybe we're getting close to the core issue of why the rebels in the eternal dimension and the hapless time-creatures wound up on the wrong side together.

Pay close attention because we are about to look at the greatest power in the universe. What I am about to talk about is the foundational issue in history, not only the history of our dimension, but the history of creation itself. From it flows all power for good in the universe. From outside it comes all power for evil. In it is the only hope for the world. Through it the world will see the human race reclaimed from futility and hatred; and what is called the supernatural realm will be cleansed and become "natural" once again. We are about to talk about a power so vital to the course of the universe that the Creator himself invaded time and space to deliver it to the creatures of this dimension.

What is this power? Submission: The willing obedience of created beings to the One who created them.

Eternal Kamikazes

So far we've focused most of our attention on the world this side of the border between time and eternity. That is understandable since few of us have had anything close to the experience of the apostles John and Paul who were privileged to peek into the world of the eternal. Our experiences are limited to time and space so it's natural that we should be inclined to focus our attention here. This is precisely why most of the Bible addresses life in this dimension. Still, there are clues about life in the eternals among the *elohim* that can be helpful as we try to piece together the relationship between the dimensions.

For the purposes of this book, I am going to start to refer to the beings created for the eternal realm as "elohim," a Hebrew world that means "mighty one" or "judge." In the right context

13

it is even used for the Creator himself, the mightiest of mighty ones. I am going to use the term in a rather narrow sense, to describe what are commonly called "angels." I am doing this so we can begin to think of these creatures apart from our Sunday school perceptions and preconceived notions about them. Sometimes a change of terminology helps us to take a fresh look at something we think is familiar.

The presence in the garden of an elohim who is fundamentally opposed to the Creator, suggests something about the conditions that govern that race. It suggests that they have the freedom to make their own choices. If God isn't in the habit of creating races of wind-up beings that he dispatches to do all kinds of evil things that are out of sync with his plan, then we have to conclude that there are "eternal free agents" who can act independently and outside of his will.

That they choose to do that tells us something else: they, that mutinous group of elohim, didn't believe God. Note that I'm not saying they didn't believe *in God,* rather that there were some of the eternal race that believed the Creator to be untruthful, fraudulent and unfair. It was that disbelief that the serpent infected the first humans with.

> "You won't die!" the serpent hissed. "God knows that your eyes will be opened when you eat it. You will become just like God, knowing everything, both good and evil."[15]

This suggests that the elohim were called on to exercise something resembling faith. Here is why I say that: if the knowledge that the eternal ones have of the Creator were exhaustive and accurate, why would any of that race have been lunatic enough to challenge the all-powerful authority of God? Consider an illustration.

I have lived in the Northwest most of my life. In 1980, May 18th to be exact, I witnessed from my window the eruption of Mount Saint Helens. In one cataclysmic instant the entire north face of the mountain blew apart, burying vast tracts of forest

---

[15] Genesis 3:4 (NLT).

and displacing much of Spirit Lake. One of those killed in the blast, Harry Truman, was buried alive near the campground there. OK, now that I've told you this, let's imagine for a moment that you could go back in time to May 17th and visit friends near the mountain. Would you accept an invitation to go camping at Spirit Lake? Based on your knowledge, probably not. You might if you were suicidal or a bit nutty, but not otherwise. The only other reason you might be inclined to do such a foolish thing is if you weren't convinced that it was foolish, if you thought I was lying or misinformed about the eruption that was about to occur.

What I'm saying is this: The only way you can have a war in the heavenlies among the eternal race that lives there is if either there were a bunch of kamikaze elohim with a death wish (whatever that might look like to an eternal being) or there were beings of that dimension that did not believe that the Creator had complete knowledge and unlimited power. As crazy as it may seem, there were apparently elohim that thought they could defeat the Creator—actually win in a war against a self-existent being with infinite power and knowledge, and against those that were submitted to him and to his will. Furthermore, they were willing to press the battle into the dimension of time and space and bring it to the doorstep of the human race.

This is why I said what I did about submission. If Adam and Eve had submitted themselves to the will of the Creator, the war in this dimension would have been over. They didn't. Rather than believe God they bought into the accusation of a rebel creature from the eternal dimension. And so the war goes on. But, as the insurgent elohim army continues to press against the human race, the central issue continues to be submission, namely who will choose to cooperate with the ultimate intention of the Creator. Since he really is the source of all power, whoever does, will win the war.

15

That issue is crucial in time and space, but it has been, and still is, just as important in the eternal dimension. A visit to the first chapter of the book of Job makes that clear.

Border Dispute

Let's take a trip to the border between the eternal dimension and time/space. That's where we find ourselves in Job 1:6.

> One day the angels came to present themselves before the LORD, and Satan the Accuser came with them.

Imagine, for a moment that the first chapter of Job is a report on your local evening news complete with video footage. The report opens with a wide shot of the border area, the blue horizon of planet earth spreading out to the right and the glittering, golden expanse of the heavenly places stretching out to the left. Thousands of elohim, creatures from the eternal dimension, are assembled before the Creator. Then, the camera angle narrows until the screen contains only two figures who are having a confrontation.

> "Where have you come from?" the LORD asked Satan. And Satan answered the LORD, "I have been going back and forth across the earth, watching everything that's going on." Then the LORD asked Satan, "Have you noticed my servant Job? He is the finest man in all the earth—a man of complete integrity. He fears God and will have nothing to do with evil."

Remember what I said about when God asks a question? It isn't because he needs information. God knew exactly where Satan had been; what's more he knew what he had been up to. Essentially he was saying, "You've been hanging around Job, haven't you? And I know why. Because you've figured out that he is completely submitted to me...unlike some people I could name." It's at that point that Satan suggests that Job is only submitted to the Creator because it's to Job's advantage. God answers, "Go ahead, snake! Knock yourself out, but you're going to find out that Job is fully submitted to me."

The game is on.

Here is where the camera angle is important. If we are not careful we can make this border dispute an issue between only two characters, God and Satan. But let's zoom out again. There are *thousands of eternal beings looking on*, hanging on every word of this disagreement between a rebel prince and the Creator of the universe. Shortly, they will be watching while one of the creatures from the time/space dimension, namely Job, demonstrates his willingness to be submitted to his Creator no matter what.

There is something to be proved here. This confrontation at the border between the dimensions suggests that in the eternals there is something about the matter of submission that needs to be settled once and for all.

In the Bible there is an interesting way in which angels doing the will of the Creator are described. They are often called "elect" or "holy" angels as if to distinguish them from other angels that aren't. The book of Job mentions in two places the apparent understanding among those that lived in ancient times that there were angels that were disobedient.[16] Even in the New Testament it is suggested that there are eternal beings that oppose God and are out of step with the Creator's plan. [17]

One enigmatic verse in the New Testament hints at the importance of the issue. It's found in Paul's first letter to the church in Corinth, chapter 11 verse 10. Here's the verse:

> So a woman should wear a covering on her head as a sign of authority because the angels are watching.

As for what Paul's instructions mean to us today, scholars are all over the map. But whether a woman should cover her head as a practice is really beside the discussion. That's not what is relevant to what we're talking about here. More to the point is this: what human beings do is of interest to the eternal

---

[16] Job 4:18 and 15:15.
[17] 2 Peter 2:4 and Jude verse 6.

ones— "the angels are watching." Second, the object of their curiosity has something to do with authority, and by implication, submission. Regardless of why the covering of the head is involved, how time/space beings deal with authority is significant to members of the eternal race.

Their fascination with what happens in the time/space dimension is evident elsewhere, too.

~ In Luke's account of the ministry of Jesus he quotes Jesus: "If anyone acknowledges me publicly here on earth, I, the Son of Man, will openly acknowledge that person in the presence of God's angels. But if anyone denies me here on earth, I will deny that person before God's angels.

~ Paul the apostle says, "We have become a spectacle to the entire world—to people and angels alike."

~ In a letter to Timothy, a young minister, Paul writes, "I solemnly command you in the presence of God and Christ Jesus and the holy angels to obey these instructions…" as though the angels should care for some reason. At least that's how Paul understood the situation between time and eternity.

There are other places, too. It's as though the events of human history are being played out in an enormous football stadium, the stands filled with observers from the eternal dimension. The bottom line is this: there is what amounts to a war going on in the infinite/eternal dimension. The whole book of Genesis has as its back-story the uprising of a rebel army of elohim aiming to achieve dominance over the creation made by a being that we in this dimension know to be infinitely powerful. To us that seems idiotic, suicidal, stupid; like a football team lining up on the tracks expecting to stop a speeding train. But remember, there are a fair number of people that don't think the Creator has infinite power, either. We may have more in common with the rebel elohim than we care to admit.

Chapter 2

Attack on Time

On the time/space side of the border between the dimensions the first of the time-creatures known as "Adam and Eve," had chosen an action with grave consequences. Some theologians liken what happened at that moment of "tree-sin" as the introduction of a disease into the human race. I don't think that goes far enough. Something deeper happened. A disease only impacts the physical things; when the first time/space creatures doubted the integrity of the Creator, as had some of the elohim, something penetrated deep and changed the core of human existence, call it their spiritual DNA.

The initial encounter with an "eternal one," was more than just casual conversation in the garden and the transmittal of a spirit microbe. While Eve was talking, and Adam listening in, the visitor from the eternal dimension was altering the "spiritual genetic material" of the race of humans, causing a change in the human spirit-genome if you will. Theologians call the result "sin nature" but we might understand it as a degradation of the genetic code of the whole human species, a mutation.

Relationship of Silence

The significance of mutations in genetic material is that they impact the physiology of a living thing, affecting how it develops and ultimately how it interacts with its environment. Furthermore, those mutations get passed down to subsequent generations. For example, deafness runs in some families. There are genes that can affect the way a person's hearing develops—some 200 forms of syndromic hereditary hearing impairment.[1] The effect of these genetic factors is congenital deafness.

That's how it works in the physical world. Could there be a parallel in our spiritual nature? What if that unwelcome visitor in the garden caused what amounted to a mutation in the spiritual life of the first humans? The effect would be passed on to every generation that followed.

Think back for a moment to the idea that we time creatures—humans—were created "amphibians" with the ability to live in the physical world as well as the eternal. If that's how we were created, it follows that we were equipped for both realms. Think of a seaplane or the amphibious crafts the military uses to transport equipment and personnel. They are designed for more than one environment, one for air and water, the other for water and land. Similarly, humans, though native to time/space, were equipped for interaction with the infinite/eternal.

But the decision to hook up with "the snake" changed all that. In the previous chapter we considered the implications of that bargain at the tree from the perspective of the elohim—as you might say, from the top. So, how does it look from ground level?

> Toward evening they heard the LORD God walking about in the garden, so they hid themselves among the trees.
>
> The LORD God called to Adam, "Where are you?"
>
> He replied, "I heard you, so I hid. I was afraid because I was naked."
>
> "Who told you that you were naked?" the LORD God asked. "Have you eaten the fruit I commanded you not to eat?"[2]

This portion of the Bible always amuses me. First, it seems a little silly for these two fruit lovers to be hiding from the

---

[1] According to the National Institute on Deafness and Other Communication Disorders.

[2] Genesis 3:11 (ESV).

Creator of the universe—like he didn't know where they were. But if that seems silly, the scene that preceded this conversation with God was hilarious:

Adam watches Eve as she takes a bite out of the fruit.

"This is good!" she says. "Try it, Adam."

Adam takes a bite. "You're right! It's delicious!"

Suddenly, he looks down and..."Whoa! I haven't got anything on here."

Meanwhile, Eve is diving into the bushes.

A few minutes ago the snake was promising these two that eating the fruit would make them wise. They eat, and what is the result of this newfound wisdom? They notice they don't have any clothes on. You have to wonder if they were very bright to begin with.

Clearly, this wasn't just about nakedness—that was obvious—this was about a change of perspective, and not for the better. Allow me to expand God's question. He was really asking something like, "So, what's the problem with being naked? That's how I brought you into this world. You've been wandering around naked for a long time. Why should it bother you now?" Here's God asking questions again. Evidently, the time/space creatures need information. What he wants them to know is, "You stopped trusting me. Earlier today you trusted me explicitly. You were completely confident that I was acting in your best interest. Just hours ago your spiritual ears were constantly tuned to my every word. You were in complete harmony with my will and purpose, but now you are confused and uncertain. We used to have an open relationship, but you ate some forbidden fruit and you're hiding in the bushes. Does that seem like a coincidence to you?"

We look at the situation and think, why didn't they just admit their mistake? Why couldn't they just regret the decision and ask to start over? Because something had changed in their spiritual DNA. They had known nothing other than the Creator's benevolent care, but still chose not to trust. At the point of this encounter with the Creator they had no idea of the consequences. He had told them that they would surely die, but they didn't believe him. What's more, as near as they could tell, they were still very much alive.

From our vantage point in history we want to warn them. Go back! Don't try to hide, for heaven's sake! Do you know where this is going to lead? Millennia of uncertainty, hatred, violence, and despair. You will peer into the jaws of hell and yearn for what you're turning from today. You and your children will wind up as food for monsters from an eternal race. On that road there is no escape from judgment, so there is no alternative to the Creator's mercy. Beg forgiveness and go back!

But they hid in the bushes. And not because they had no clothes. It was because there was a deconstruction of the interface between the time/space beings and the Creator (2 Corinthians 5:2-4). In essence, they had orphaned themselves from their Father.

It was at that time that what we know as "prayer" became necessary.

The Birth of Prayer

Prayer has been variously described as communication with God and a "hotline" to heaven. Both descriptions are true, although they fall short of grasping what prayer really is: the echo of the rich relationship that once existed between time/space creatures and their Creator; a pale image of the relationship that once was before the mutation of human spiritual DNA. Calling it an "echo" and a "pale image" doesn't make prayer unimportant; to the contrary, it means that it is vital. It is not just a hotline; it is a lifeline.

Perhaps an illustration will help.

The Internet has become an important tool today. The technology is vital for disseminating information. Commerce, communication, and research have come to depend on it. In general, there are two ways of accessing the Internet. First, there is what's called "broadband" which features a constant connection to the net. If your computer is on, you're on the Internet—a continual connection. The other is called "dial-up." This option requires the computer user to access the Internet through their telephone line. When you want to use the net you have to, in essence, call it, wait for it to answer, and only then are you connected to the Internet.

As a recent convert to broadband I can tell you that I much prefer it to dial-up. Whenever I want to look something up, send an e-mail, or visit a web site, I just punch a few keys and—poof—I'm there! Dial-up meant that I had to stop what I was doing, "go online" wait for things to download, upload, reload…whatever…and only then was I connected.

It was the broadband kind of relationship with the Creator that was lost in the garden. The "always on" connection with God was broken, leaving the time-creatures with the spiritual equivalent of dial-up, namely prayer. Before, humans were of one mind with the Creator because they lived in agreement with him, never questioning or doubting. Until the encounter with the serpent, there appears to have been almost a family relationship across the boundary of the dimensions. The relationship was assumed, like children who have an intuitive sense of what their parents want, and act in accordance with those wishes.

For His part, the Creator knew that His presence and relationship was always welcome. But after humans disconnected themselves from that relationship, things were different. The time creatures no longer welcomed the Creator. How do we know that? They hid from him.

My children are grown and live on their own now. Still, they know that they are always welcome in our house. We leave a key for them to use when they need to get in; our son never gave his house key back when he moved out. Our kids assume, rightly, that they are always welcome in our house. The reverse is not true. We don't have a key to their house that we use whenever we want. We wait for our kids to invite us to enter their home. We don't assume that all times are good times to go barging in. We wait for an invitation.

It appears that what happened in Genesis is like that. Once the time-creatures doubted His integrity and trustworthiness, the Creator became like a parent whose children had moved out. At that point He began to wait for an invitation to become involved in their lives. He didn't just barge in, although barging doesn't seem to have been the pattern anyhow.

There is a further complication. Because humans were no longer enabled to access the other dimension, they were no longer synchronized with it. Previously, there was what might be called an instinctive awareness of how things should be. But, having terminated the connection, the signal from the far side of the dimensional barrier became garbled. The result, where prayer is concerned, is that when humans extend an invitation to the Creator to intervene across the dimensional barrier, the request may not be in sync with the flow of creation. Invitations (what we call prayers) were, and still are, frequently out of harmony with the creative intent of the universe and therefore inappropriate. Not only did the Creator begin to wait for His creatures to invite His involvement in their world, He also needed to wait for them to recover a sense of his heart when they asked—to figure out what He would want rather than ask for what would be contrary to His nature.

James and John, two of Jesus disciples whom he nicknamed, "sons of thunder," make a good case in point. Having been rejected by a certain city they suggested that they should call fire to rain down on the town. Jesus response? He scolded them for asking for something that was outside of God's will. In short, God not only waits to be invited, He waits for an invitation He can accept (1 John 5:14). Occasionally, we get it right. Often, like James and John, we don't.

That is quite different from the open, "broadband" relationship that was originally hard-wired into the human spirit. The good news is the Creator intends to reestablish that old relationship. Meanwhile, we time-creatures have a dial-up connection available…and the circuits are never busy.

Unilateral Involvement

Don't get the idea that the encounter between humans and the elohim resulted in the withdrawal of the Creator from the earth dimension. According to the written record of these things, He appears to maintain a level of involvement that he exercises when ultimate destiny hangs in the balance.

In the last part of the third chapter of Genesis, the Creator begins to download the program that will be needed to re-synchronize the dimensions. That, after all, is what has happened in the encounter between the two races: the dimensions stopped functioning in harmony. The symbiotic relationship (a relationship of mutual benefit) between temporal and eternal creatures became parasitic as the elohim attempted to forcibly extract life from humans. Rather than allow that to continue, the Creator stepped in and took remedial action. He dealt decisively with the actual behavior that was out of sync with the flow of creation—a serious spanking. The eternal creature was humiliated—"you will grovel in the dust"—and the humans were given a description of the life that awaited them now that they had traded away their ability to function across the dimensions.

The most important part of that "spanking" is the first mention of a person called "The Seed." During the Creator's reprimand of the snake He says,

> And I will put enmity, between you and the woman, and between your seed and her *seed*; He shall bruise you on the head, and you shall bruise him on the heel.[3]

Notice the word "seed" is used twice in this sentence. I've italicized one of them because it is used differently from the other. The first use refers to the serpent and his offspring, which are beings, descendants carrying his figurative DNA.

---

[3] Genesis 3:15 (NASB).

The important thing is that "seed" in this first case refers to *many* and that they will have similar qualities to him.

The second time the word is used it refers not to many, but to one. Do you see it? "*He* will bruise your head..." In some translations the word is "crush," but the important thing is that it is a single person. Somebody, sometime will deal a death blow to the leader of this elohim rebellion. A blow to the head is deadly. This mention of "The Seed" suggests—promises—that somebody will repair the breach of relationship in the eternal and temporal dimensions, essentially undo what the serpent has done, and restore the bi-dimensional life of the human race.

From the moment of that announcement, the machinery was in motion toward restoration. The machinery is still in motion, although "The Seed" is no longer the man of mystery he once was. Hang on to that. We'll come back to it.

Soliloquy

Probably the most famous soliloquy in all of theatre is from Shakespeare's *Hamlet*. The title character steps forward on the stage as though he is thinking out loud and says, "To be or not to be, that is the question..." Shakespeare includes this scene of Hamlet talking to himself because Hamlet's words are important to the audience who needs to know what he is thinking. What he says "to himself" reveals the plot. In Genesis, God does something similar. As a matter of fact, He does it three times in Genesis, and each time He describes an important intervention He is about to undertake relative to the operation of the interface between the dimensions. These soliloquies are signals that there is about to be a significant revelation of God's purposes and a momentous change in the status quo—no more business as usual.

The first intervention, in the third chapter, is in response to the elohim insurgency and the damage it has done to the spiritual DNA of the time-creatures. Listen to the Creator's soliloquy, and then note His action:

Then the LORD God said, "The people have become as we are, knowing everything, both good and evil. What if they eat the fruit of the tree of life? Then they will live forever!" So the LORD God banished Adam and his wife from the Garden of Eden, and He sent Adam out to cultivate the ground from which He had been made. After banishing them from the garden, the LORD God stationed mighty angelic beings to the east of Eden. And a flaming sword flashed back and forth, guarding the way to the tree of life.[4]

Here is that tree I mentioned in the last chapter, the tree of life. Whether it was a tree with magic fruit (the prototype for all the stories we've ever read about fountains of youth) or it amounted to the opening between the dimensions we don't know. I'm a little bothered by the "magic fruit" hypothesis, but the record does say it was a tree. Whatever it was, the implication is that time-creatures, at that moment had at their disposal a means of interacting with the eternal dimension.

But also at this moment in the story, as the Creator steps forward on the stage of history, there's a problem: humans are estranged from Him and out of sync with the rhythms of creation. Moreover, there are already a significant number of creatures with that same problem living in the eternal dimension, the rebellious elohim. What was the Creator to do? Leave the human race in its broken condition and let its creatures spend eternity practicing that brokenness—imagine a Hitler, or a Stalin, living forever unrestrained. Not only that, without intervention, the battle between creatures submitted to the creative impulse of God and those who chose rebellion would be fought eternally across the dimensions.

Not so good.

No, the human race needed an overhaul and, appropriately enough for time-creatures, the time to see it done. The Creator closes the door on eternity putting it under the protection of loyal elohim. Though created to be spiritual amphibians, the time creatures become stranded in the time/space dimension;

---

[4] Genesis 3:22.

27

and all because of the mutation of their spiritual DNA and their hapless alliance with the extraterrestrial[5] rebels.

There are two reasons you guard a doorway. One is, to prevent entry—to keep undesirable people out; the other reason is to protect the doorway for future use at the right time. The elohim guards (probably two of them, but it's not clearly stated here) were assigned to preserve a right of access for the human race, in anticipation of a time when that race would be reconciled with its Creator and synchronized with His creative intent—fit company for the loyal elohim.

This is a good time to stop and make note of something. As the epic of creation unfolds the Creator is inserting markers into the chronicles of human history as evidence of His ongoing project of restoration. More than just written records, these markers are designed to be symbolic, existing outside of language. For example, the image of a snake has become synonymous with the encroachment of evil. Later, a rainbow will be given symbolic meaning, as will these two loyal elohim that, according to the record, are protecting the interface between the dimensions.

The first such marker to be mentioned is "The Seed". Here, at the very beginning, is a historical symbol anticipating the future response of the Creator to the rebellion that spilled out of the eternal dimension and into the temporal world. The Seed is to be the means through which that is to happen. The Seed will become a metaphor for restoration.

But other markers are being laid down. After noting the promise of "The Seed," Genesis mentions that the Creator makes an answer to the nakedness of the humans. Remember, their physical nudity isn't the real issue. The issue is disconnectedness from their intended place in the created universe. Nevertheless, God covers their physical nakedness

---

[5] Extraterrestrial usually refers to some kind of space alien. In this context I'm using the term to describe a being not native to the time-space dimension, as well as to the planet that exists in it.

when He "made clothing of animal skins for Adam and his wife."

Here is a first: dead animals. Imagine for a moment an absolutely harmonious environment where none of the inhabitants have a "killer instinct." That was the condition in the embryonic world described in Genesis—death doesn't seem to have been a part of it. The record notes that in this idyllic world the humans even gave names to the animals. What would be the impact of two of these docile creatures killed and skinned where the humans could find them? What message would the humans gather from this? What should we make of it, as we observe these events through the eyes of history? Something about death and blood being necessary for spiritual nakedness to be covered. This marker, and the others, will be picked up later as God isolates a segment of the human race—we call them Israelites—to illustrate for time-creatures everywhere what it means to be submitted to the Creator. Furthermore, it will be through that portion of the race that the Creator will describe the reunification of creation.

As history unfolds, the Hebrew nation will develop a system of animal sacrifice, ostensibly via specific instructions to a man named Moses from the very Creator that killed the animals in the garden. Furthermore, the man Moses will be given the plans for a unique piece of furniture to be used in the Hebrew worship rites. You may have seen the movie *Raiders of the Lost Ark*. The film is about the discovery of that piece of furniture, the fabled Ark of the Covenant. Assuming the prop department for the film did their homework, the ark is a box, made of gold. Attached to the top of the box, arched over it like sentries, are two angelic beings. Remind you of anything? Remember the loyal elohim guarding the way to the eternal dimension? Lest we forget about them and the doorway they are guarding, the Creator has inserted a reminder, a marker, into history.

These things are not coincidental. And there are many more such markers.

The Attack

Let's revisit the scene of the crime where the captain of the rebel elohim duped the time-creatures into complicity. There is a strategy in this duplicitous attack on human liberty. The rebels had intended to hijack the entire race and win them en masse to the rebel cause. Evidently, the serpent assumed that breaking the link between the Creator and the time-creatures would produce what amounted to a race of drones, helplessly bound to a new master, namely him. Fortunately, it wasn't that easy.

When Adam and Eve chose to rebel and to doubt the character of the Creator, it interrupted their amphibious capabilities and those of their descendents (that spiritual mutation, remember) but it didn't render inoperative their future freedom to choose. The Creator did not design the choice-making ability of humans to be contingent on Him. It was designed to be exercised remotely—even independently. The first humans used their freedom foolishly and paid dearly for it. They stumbled outside the rhythm/flow of the universe so they no longer acted innately and intuitively in harmony with it—they severed the "broadband" relationship with the Creator. But they retained the essential quality of freedom. One bad, even calamitous, decision did not render future choices impossible. On a case-by-case basis the time-creatures could still choose to submit.

One has to wonder if that was a surprise to the rebels. Perhaps they thought the war would be won with a single strike against the spirit of the time-creatures. If so, they misjudged. Although it's hard to imagine the world of the elohim—a non-linear realm—it is at least possible that reasoned decisions in an eternal environment are, in fact, eternal decisions, once made they are made forever. If that is the case, perhaps the elohim didn't understand the characteristics of creation in the temporal dimension and the multi-faceted nature of the race that is native to it.

A look at the blueprint of human beings will be helpful here.

In the New Testament, Paul the Apostle writes, "Now may the God of peace sanctify you *entirely;* and may your spirit and soul and body be preserved *complete...*"[6] I've italicized two words because 'entirely' and 'complete' suggest that the apostle views whole human beings (in contrast to partial ones, I suppose) as being triplex in nature; body, soul and spirit.

The body, of course, is the vehicle—the hardware—that actually interfaces with time and space. It is made of the same stuff as the rest of the tangible universe. Humans are equipped with senses—sight, hearing, touch, smell and taste—to actually interact with the material world.

The soul is like the body's navigation system. It is the component of our nature that we use to interpret our relationship with this dimension and to interact with it, and with creatures like ourselves that live here. Traditionally, our soul is said to be the seat of our mind, will, and emotions. In short, it is our personality and decision-making apparatus.

Overlapping with the soul, but distinct from it, is our spirit—what the Bible metaphorically calls the *breath.* The spirit is the part of us that was designed to be hardwired to the Creator and to interface with the infinite/eternal part of creation. Think of it as the navigation system for the other dimension, the non-tangible one. At first, when humans (with their amphibious qualities intact) were at liberty to traverse between dimensions, it would have been the spirit that made the interaction possible.

Where our spirit overlaps with our soul is important because it overlaps at the point of our *will*, that part of us that makes decisions. For the first of our race, and for all who followed (including you and me) that decision apparatus was supposed to be governed by the spirit. It wasn't intended to be activated by the body and soul. That may explain why the human spirit, specifically the human will, was the target that

---

[6] 1 Thessalonians 5:23 (NASB).

the invader in the garden aimed at. It may also explain why humans seem so inclined to continue to respond to the invader.

The inclination to bond with an enemy is not unheard of. In 1973 two robbers attempted to hold up a bank in Stockholm. Almost immediately, the robbery went awry and the bandits wound up taking four bank employees hostage, one man and three women, in the bank's vault. Amazingly, after 131 days of captivity, the hostages resisted rescue and declared a fondness for their captors!

Bizarre.

Psychologists explain the phenomenon as a survival skill that people in threatening situations adopt in order to cope with the stress of being vulnerable. It was not unheard of before 1973, but the event in Sweden was so widely publicized and the attitude of the hostages so remarkable that the incident caused the condition to be referred to as "Stockholm Syndrome." The kidnap of Patty Hearst by the Symbionese Liberation Army and later, Elizabeth Smart made the syndrome notorious. Most recently, the televised denunciations of hostages in the Mid-East prompt discussions of the subject.

I bring this up here because it is a good illustration of what happened as a result of the attack on the human race perpetrated by "the serpent." Though Satan's malevolent intentions seem pretty clear, still humans gravitate toward him in a process we call temptation.

Although the attack on the human spirit did not leave the time-race helpless, it did leave the humans handicapped—casualties of war. The net effect of a darkened spirit was that humans were suddenly unable to perceive beyond the world of sight and sound, or clearly discern the voice of their Creator. No longer endowed with the ability to interact freely with the infinite/eternal dimension, they were forced to make do with senses suited only to time/space: eyes, ears, and hands; mind, will, and emotions—spirit off-line, soul and body leading the way. That spelled trouble. Once they decided God wasn't to be trusted, who did that leave in charge? Them, of course. With their spirit disconnected and no longer in command of their lives, there was no way to discern the rhythm of the universe, much less act in harmony with it. That was the condition that was passed down through the corrupted spiritual genome of the human race.

To look at it another way, you could think of the spirit as a radio COM link capable of multiple frequencies, able to communicate on the time/space frequency and also on the frequency of the Creator. The incident in the garden "fried" the channel used for communication with eternity. The result was that the soul, no longer linked to eternity, began to make its own way, functioning independently of the spirit, unwilling and unable to respond to the spirit's direction. The activity of the independent soul is impulsive, drinking deeply from the tainted well of lust, pride and sensuality. It ignores the warnings of the spirit because its default frequency has been changed from the eternal channel to the channel of time/space.

Here, again is where the power of submission becomes clear. The Creator intended that both dimensions, and their respective races, exist "in sync" with Him and by extension, with each other. That is the core definition of submission. The soul (physical wants and emotional tendencies) was designed to be under the authority of the spirit, which, if tuned properly, was supposed to be responding to the Creator.

The soul—that stubborn little bundle of mind, will and emotion—is the part of Adam and Eve's character that triggered the forbidden fruit incident in the first place. The initial deception was aimed at the mind and emotions (Genesis 3:1-5), physical senses sweetened the bargain (verse 6), then, stumbling stupidly after physical appetites, the will portion of the human soul inked the deal. Adam and Eve traded away the freedom that came from being a whole unit, spirit, soul, and body, at the tree of knowledge.

Every generation since has instinctively yearned for restored relationship. Actually, there is a sense in which the biblical narrative is like the story of lovers separated by the winds of war. Wars are all about victory and loss, anxiety and grief, and separation. But wars are also about hope and anticipation. Anyone that has ever bid farewell to a loved one headed off to war knows the sorrow of parting, and anyone who has welcomed a loved one home knows the joy of reunion. It is these conflicting emotions that are playing out between the principal actors in the drama of the ages. As the war between the rebels of heaven impacts the world of time and space, the yearning of the heart of God grows more intense, as does the yearning of all creation. The apostle Paul reminds us that all creation anticipates the *summing up of all things*. Moreover, we have to assume that includes the loyal and submissive elohim, what the Bible calls the holy angels who, as I suggested previously, were designed to be in partnership with human beings.

War on Two Fronts

So, the warfare of the universe plays out. On one side the Creator plans and executes a fitting response to the rebellion; the loyal elohim await specific instructions even as they yearn for the full revelation of what human beings were to eventually become and for an understanding of their own complimentary role with them. The humans quietly, instinctively long for the wholeness that was lost in the garden.

Meanwhile, the rebels are continuing to press their assault on creation.

The battle for dominance over creation, including time/space and the race that lives there is to be fought on two fronts. One is purely an offensive, aimed at assimilating these unfamiliar time/space beings. The other is preemptive, an effort to circumvent the Creator's plan to ultimately destroy the rebellion through the use of a secret weapon He called "the Seed."

First, the offensive strategy.

There is a suggestion that the insurgency is forced to change its tactics in response to the actions of the Creator. I think that they misjudged the vulnerability of the time-creatures, thinking that to win the cooperation of the first two was to secure their blind obedience and also the submission of the rest of the time creatures that were to follow. But that's not what happened. Having never encountered time-creatures before, the enemy commanders have learned something: a decision made in time isn't like a decision in eternity, it isn't a once and for all proposition. Furthermore, the numbers are in constant flux. New time-creatures are created seemingly at the whim of older time-creatures, each new generation with the same capacity for decision making—freedom to choose—that their ancestors had. Very disconcerting. So how does an angelic insurgency attack such a moving target? Let's try to picture a high-level meeting of rebel strategists. The cameras are rolling again. The scene opens on a dozen or so dark angels that have gathered around a large table. A map of the world hangs on the wall. There are concentric circles drawn on it emanating from a central point somewhere near the modern city of Baghdad. Let's listen in as the leader, newly nicknamed *the Snake*, lays out a plan:

> *OK, the time-creatures aren't as vulnerable as first thought. Their freedom to choose remains intact even though they are no longer free to navigate in the eternal realm. If we can't assimilate the race in its entirety, we'll have to capture it one being at a time. That's still doable. We already proved we can alter them by enticing their will. We will just continue to do that one generation at a time, combine them into larger units and use those to destroy the ones we can't alter. We can influence them against one another. It can be done.*

The fourth chapter of Genesis picks up the story of the second generation of the time creatures. It also illustrates a new tactical approach by the rebel elohim.

As Genesis 4 begins we learn that Adam and Eve have become parents. Their first son, Cain by name, has a knack for making things grow. Undoubtedly it was hard work, God said

35

it would be, but apparently Cain took to it naturally. Abel, the other son, was more drawn to the animal world, tending to the herds.

It should be noted that there were other children in the family. We find that out in a few verses when Cain gets sent away and meets up with somebody to marry. Yes, that means that he married his sister, or at least a close cousin, but at that early stage there weren't any other options.

Anyhow, back in verse three it says,

> So it came about in the course of time that Cain brought an offering to the LORD of the fruit of the ground. Abel, on his part also brought of the firstlings of his flock and of their fat portions And the LORD had regard for Abel and for his offering; but for Cain and for his offering He had no regard. So Cain became very angry and his countenance fell.

Verse three introduces us to the kids at a time when they have grown old enough to work and follow directions. This is important because some scholars surmise that three things are suggested by the verses you just read. First, that the offering Cain and Abel bring wasn't just a random thing. Some translations begin the verses by saying, "at the end of days," or "in the fullness of time" the boys brought their offering, implying that a specific time for offerings had been established. In other words, the boys were to be following instructions about that. Secondly, notice that they "brought" an offering. We can assume that they didn't pack up their animals and vegetables and start wandering aimlessly about without knowing where they were going. There was apparently a place to bring the offerings to. We aren't told exactly where, but Cain and Abel bring their offering to some fixed place. Personally, I think it was somewhere near the doorway to the tree of life, but I wasn't there, so I can't be sure. Finally, the nature of the offering may also have been part of the instruction to the sons, which explains why Cain was in trouble for bringing vegetables.

In the previous chapter I mentioned that God had begun leaving clues and markers in human history in order to point toward his ultimate plan for healing the divide between He and His creation. The first such marker was the mention of "the seed." The placement of the what the Bible calls "cherubim" as guards to the access point to eternity will become another. This business of offerings is yet another marker. Perhaps Abel's offering was more appropriate than Cain's because God wanted to make sure the human race would remember what it costs to make up for disobedience. Remember those animals that paid for Adam and Eve's first suit of clothes at the cost of their lives? It is not unlikely that the nature of an offering was important because it was to serve as a reminder of that. Vegetables don't tell the story of the cost of disobedience. Shedding the blood of innocent animals makes a more vivid point. Bringing offerings as a sign of submission and cooperation was to be a part of God's ultimate plan of restoration and the marker was set right here.

A Matter of Choice

But Cain chose not to follow the rules. Rather than bring an offering from the flock, a reminder of the cost of disobedience, he worked his hardest and offered God the produce of his own labor. He brought stuff that had grown out of the very ground that God had told Adam was cursed. Another poor choice in Adam's family.

You can see the covert operation behind this. As Eve (and Adam) were to have avoided the tree in the garden, so Cain was to have demonstrated his submission to the Creator, by bringing the appropriate offering. Somewhere along the line Cain thought he had a better idea just as his parents had. Do you have to wonder where he got the idea, or rather from whom?

But remember freedom to choose is a quality that remains active in every human and, although choices can sometimes have far-reaching consequences, time-creatures still retain the ability to make them. That's why the Creator visits Cain, the disobedient son, and tries to nudge him to better use that freedom, and as He does, teaches us, too. The encounter is tender, almost fatherly:

> "Why are you so angry?" the LORD asked him. "Why do you look so dejected? You will be accepted if you respond in the right way. But if you refuse to respond correctly, then watch out! Sin is waiting to attack and destroy you, and you must subdue it."[7]

In this case, like a heavenly Father, the Creator corrects this second generation human. He explains the importance of submission. He tells Cain that when you walk in submission to your spiritual heritage you are accepted. On the other hand, if you choose disobedience, you are vulnerable to an attack from the dark side. God in these few verses makes it clear that he knows exactly how the rebels have switched their strategy. He also makes it clear that human choice properly applied can neutralize an enemy attack. Knowing that, how did Cain do? Not so good.

> Later Cain suggested to his brother, Abel, "Let's go out into the fields." And while they were there, Cain attacked and killed his brother.
>
> Afterward the LORD asked Cain, "Where is your brother? Where is Abel?"
>
> "I don't know!" Cain retorted. "Am I supposed to keep track of him wherever he goes?"[8]

If Adam and Eve ever talked to their sons about the time in the garden when the Creator asked them a question, Cain apparently didn't remember that when God asks you something, you're the one who is about to learn. He learned that he had just fallen prey to the strategy of the rebel elohim. As a result he gets sent out to make his own way in the world.

---

[7] Genesis 4:6-7 (NLT).
[8] Verses 6-9.

If you read on, the rest of Genesis 4 and through Genesis 5, you see the strategy play out. Generation after generation the time-creatures wrestle with the issue of submission and the war within the ranks of the elohim spills over into time and space through the creatures who are native to that dimension.

But the stakes are about to get even higher. The enemy is about to attempt a preemptive strike against the holy ones of God.

Chapter 3

Plan B

When the elohim launched their first assault into time and space, the target was the human spirit. That was Plan A. Having not been wholly successful, they went to the war room and instituted Plan B.

The first prong of Plan B attempts to use human will and free choice to the advantage of the insurgency. The ongoing battle in the war between the dimensions will not be fought by one isolated commando set to destroy two people, it will be fought by an army of rebellious angels. The human race will experience a relentless battering of the soul as, one by one, every human creature will have to decide whether to submit to the Creator's intended design or to operate completely in the time/space dimension as a pawn of the rebellion.

The second prong of Plan B is a preemptive strike. Let's visit the war room again as the insurgents consider the implications of the Creator's remarks about a secret weapon that He intends to use to destroy the rebel commander and wipe out his army, a weapon drawn from within the time dimension, "The Seed." Based on what the insurgency has witnessed so far, a threat from the time-creatures doesn't seem like much of a threat. Still, the Snake (for so he has come to be known) isn't about to take chances, hence he considers his options. Leaning toward his officers he speaks...

There is one worrisome thing, though. It appears the Creator intends to use genetics to reactivate the spirit-life of the humans and reconnect the dimensions. So far the human creatures don't seem to pose much of a threat, yet I don't want to underestimate the Creator. This "Seed" business should be stopped. We must do whatever we can to interrupt that whole plan. I propose that we launch another attack, not just in the time/space dimension, but on the time/space dimension. We will scramble the human genetic code. That should put an end to any counterstrike from within the tangible world. We'll breed out the threat so there can be no "seed" from the human race.

I can imagine a murmur rising from among the ranks. *How do we do that?* The question begs for an answer. The Snake smiles.

You're going to like this. We'll assemble an army and make an amphibious landing in the time dimension. I've seen the time creatures. The ones who bear the seed of their race are quite attractive. The one I spoke with was naïve, too. It's a useful combination that I'm certain our elohim can exploit. We will create a new race, which will be useless to the Creator for whatever purpose He had intended.

The intention of the rebel elohim is more insidious than you can imagine—something akin to mass rape. The results will become the stuff of legend—some will say myth.

Invasion

Genesis 6 is something of an enigma among scholars. Some say it is about the righteous line of Seth, the child that Eve bore as a replacement for her murdered son, Abel. They speculate it is about how Seth's kin had forbidden relationships with the unrighteous offspring of Cain. Others say that it is the story of an amphibious landing of rebel angels who use their ability to operate in the material world for purposes of corruption and destruction.

You already know where we come down on the issue. The first four verses of the chapter explain why.

When the human population began to grow rapidly on the earth, *the sons of God* saw the beautiful women of the human race and took any they wanted as their wives. Then the LORD said, "My Spirit will not put up with humans for such a long time, for they are only mortal flesh. In the future, they will live no more than 120 years."

In those days, and even afterward, giants lived on the earth, for whenever the *sons of God* had intercourse with human women, they gave birth to children who became the heroes mentioned in legends of old. (Genesis 6:1-4 NLT)

I've italicized a phrase that appears twice in this description, "the sons of God." Who were these people? As I said before, some believe them to be men from Seth's lineage. If that's so, we're left to conclude that Seth invariably fathered lots of nice boys but managed to father some pretty homely girls that were apparently of little interest to his male descendents. That is why the guys started chasing after the girls from the line of Cain who had the genetic good fortune to be beautiful.

But what if what's going on here is precisely what it appears to be? What if Genesis is using a term that we are to understand to mean *elohim,* in this case rebel angels? Let's visit the book of Job again. As you recall, in Job there was an encounter at the border of the dimensions between the Snake and the Creator. Remember who was there? Angels. In Job they are called "the sons of God," the same term that shows up in Genesis 6. It is used in Job 1:6; 2:1; and 38:7. Many versions of the Bible simply translate the term "angels."

Scholars differ somewhat on when Job was written. Some say it pre-dated the book of Genesis, which is regarded as penned by Moses. Others say it came after Genesis, or was contemporary to it, perhaps also written by Moses. Either way, the term "sons of God" would have been familiar enough that it could be consistently applied in the two works. Furthermore, what we would call a "spirit-being" interpretation in Genesis is consistent with what comes next, an account of a supernatural race that emerged from the coming together of the "sons of God" and the "daughters of men."

The New Living Translation's treatment of that supernatural race is to simply call them "giants." Many other translations use a rendering of the Hebrew word, *Nephilim*, a word that eventually came into common usage and was understood to mean any mighty warriors of enormous size.[1] Interestingly, the term comes from a root that means, "to fall." Various understandings of the word are that these big people were strong and that when they attacked (fell upon) someone, you could be certain the victim would fall before them. Another thought is that people would just fall down before these giants because they were bullies and tyrants. Personally, I like another understanding of the word, namely that these were *fallen creatures*, a product of the amphibious assault of fallen angels.

I have suggested in the prologue that much fantasy and legend that has been attributed to human creativity, is actually cultural memory at work, and that the human race maintains a shared recollection of these events. Polytheistic cultures nearly all imagine warfare among "the gods" and the gods having interaction with humans, sometimes even having human

---

[1] The New English Translation (NET Bible) includes this note on Genesis 6: The Hebrew word נְפִילִים (nᵉfilim) is simply transliterated here, because the meaning of the term is uncertain. According to the text, the Nephilim became mighty warriors and gained great fame in the antediluvian world. The text may imply they were the offspring of the sexual union of the "sons of God" and the "daughters of humankind" (Genesis 6:2), but it stops short of saying this in a direct manner. The Nephilim are mentioned in the OT only here and in Numbers 13:33, where it is stated that they were giants (thus KJV, TEV, NLT "giants" here). The narrator observes that the Anakites of Canaan were descendants of the Nephilim. Certainly these later Anakite Nephilim could not be descendants of the antediluvian Nephilim.

consorts.[2] This concept of the relationship between the dimensions fits very well with the propaganda machine of the rebellion—it isn't hard to imagine the rebel elohim styling themselves as gods among the time-creatures. Furthermore, many cultures record in their mythology the existence of a particular kind of spirit-being called an *incubus* which was a "lascivious male demon said to possess mortal women as they sleep [for the purpose of intercourse] and to be responsible for the birth of demons, witches, and deformed children. According to one legend the incubus and his female counterpart, the succubus, were fallen angels." [3]

The bottom line is that there is good reason to take what it says in Genesis 6 at face value. Renegade Angels used their free will and innate ability to breach the border between the dimensions and take on a physical form. Angels do that throughout the Bible. These angels invaded time and space and somehow, in ways that we don't fully understand, created a hybrid race by altering human DNA.

Small wonder that the Creator is not happy with this development.

Giant Problem

The outcome of the rebel attack was grievous to the Creator. Not only that, He was growing impatient. That's what is meant in the verses above when God says, "My Spirit will not put up with humans…" Let me paraphrase his comments in a way that may make it a little clearer. I'll borrow from the script of nearly every parent of pre-schoolers. Have you ever said anything like this?

---

[2] In Greek mythology, for example, Zeus has a tragic relationship with a beautiful mortal woman named Semele.

[3] "Incubus." The Columbia Electronic Encyclopedia, Sixth Edition. Columbia University Press., 2003. *Answers.com* 21 Feb. 2006. http://www.answers.com/topic/incubus.

"I have just about had it with you kids! You are being naughty. I'm going to count to FIVE so you better straighten up or…pow! …ONE! TWO! THREE…"

That's pretty much what the Creator was saying although on a much grander scale: "I'm not going to put up with the human race much longer. They're running amok in their flesh. I'm going to give them 120 years and then I'm through with them!" Note he's not talking about human lifespan here (the above NLT translation notwithstanding) he's talking about how long before he deals decisively with this race of violent, morally corrupt people.

We'll get to those consequences in a bit, but first let's pause for a status report from "battlefield earth." From the look of things, the elohim invasion has had its planned result, the corruption of the human seed. The race of time-creatures yielded without a fight. With the exception of one man and his family, the corruption was so thorough that the race of time natives became polluted body and soul. They used their will—freedom to choose—to yield their mind and emotions to their body, what the Bible calls "the flesh," to the extent that their sexual appetites were unrestrained. The outcome included a monstrous hybrid race that became legendary in many cultures throughout history. The temporal dimension was in ruins. Here's how the Bible puts it:

> Now the LORD observed the extent of the people's wickedness, and he saw that all their thoughts were consistently and totally evil. So the LORD was sorry he had ever made them. It broke his heart. And the LORD said, "I will completely wipe out this human race that I have created. Yes, and I will destroy all the animals and birds, too. I am sorry I ever made them." But Noah found favor with the LORD.[4]

---

[4] Genesis 6:5-8.

One could assume that the rebels have won the war if it weren't for that last sentence, "But Noah found favor with LORD." Apparently, the war isn't over at all.

Something has happened in the scenario here in chapter 6 that should cause us to take notice. It is God's presence in the scene. Do you remember the last time the Creator stepped forward on the stage of human history and made a speech? It was just before He put under armed guard the gateway to the timeless section of the universe, effectively excluding the fallen race of time-creatures—disobedient and unsubmitted—from the eternal dimension. He placed a new limitation on them.

Now, another catastrophe has occurred in the time/space world. A substantial part of two races, one from the non-spatial world and the other from the temporal dimension demonstrate that they are totally out of harmony with the intentions of creation. In short, among both created races there are significant numbers that have abandoned cooperation with God. There are, among the elohim, a substantial portion who have remained loyal, but among the time-creatures all have abandoned submission, with one exception.

What follows in the story is God's singling out of Noah and a conversation that the Creator has with him; something about building a large boat, which is what the Creator had in mind when he announced His impatience with the human race. How long do you think it might take to build a boat 450 feet long and 45 feet high? My guess is about 120 years. If it had been left to me, considerably longer.

Undoubtedly, you know the story from your days in Sunday school. Noah packs up his family along with a literal boatload of animals that wandered into town from who knows where. When the last ones arrive, there is a clap of thunder and it starts to rain and doesn't stop until the world is awash and all of Noah's neighbors, including the Nephilim, are left to tread water.

This is the consequence of not being in harmony with creation. God destroys the bulk of the human race and starts fresh with one family he salvages from among the scum of the earth. And what was the quality that made the Noah family fit for a 40-day cruise? Submission. They were in harmony with the purposes of creation.

They Didn't See It Coming

A worldwide deluge amounts to a colossal spanking of the human race, and the monstrous hybrid race that lived among them.

Now what? The insurgency's plan failed. They apparently didn't expect the annihilation of most of the beings living in the time/space world. Rebel army routed, right? And the time-creatures start over again. But here's a question that we should be asking. What's to keep the elohim from doing it again?

Do you get the feeling that there is another shoe that is about to drop?

The last time the Creator made a speech he meted out consequences in three directions. He cursed the elohim commander, limiting his activity in the time/space dimension. Then he pronounced to the time-creatures the penalties to be paid by them—they and the race that was to descend from them. Finally, he barred any human access into the eternal dimension until the time-creatures could be restored to harmony with their original design.

Here, in the days of Noah, a similar thing happens. God makes a speech. Consequences for the human race: the flood and the destruction of all but one submitted family. But what about the rebels? No consequences for the invaders?

I think there were. Although the penalty isn't clearly spelled out here, the cost of the attack on human DNA was staggering for the elohim. It forced a change in rebel strategy that persists to this day. Just as there were limitations placed on the time-creatures, there was a penalty to be paid by the elohim in both situations, too. And my guess is that the rebels didn't see this one coming, either.

What that penalty was for the elohim is less clear than for the time-creatures, but not less significant. Notice something interesting about the activity of eternal beings after the days of Noah. After the flood, when there are specific appearances of the elohim in time/space they are always on a mission from the Creator. They are always doing His bidding and carrying out His instructions. In other words, we only see *submitted* eternal-ones making the trip into the world of the time-creatures. It appears only they still have a "backstage pass" into time and space. Rebel angels don't *materialize* in time/space any more. There are only two apparent exceptions, but I don't think they are really exceptions.

The first is the situation when Jesus (The Seed) is tempted by the Devil. The account appears in the fourth chapter of both Matthew and Luke's gospel and in the first chapter of Mark's. Here is what is written in the New Living Translation:

~ Then the Devil came to Him... (Matthew 4:1)

~ He was...being tempted by the Devil. (Luke 4:2)

~ ...the Devil tempted Him for forty days. (Mark 1:13)

Interestingly, the word for the rebel commander is different in each account. Matthew calls him "the tempter," Mark, "the adversary" and finally, Luke calls him "the accuser," all very appropriate descriptions of this fallen angel.

The question is, in what form did the tempter, the accuser, the adversary try to outwit The Seed? Based on the biblical accounts, it is said he "came" or he "tempted." It does not say, "he appeared." The notion that this rebel elohim was present in a material form is only suggested in that he "takes" Jesus variously to the temple and to a high mountain. The mechanics of those excursions—how Jesus came to be in those places—aren't clearly stated. If His visit to the highest tower of the Jerusalem temple or to a high mountain were literal, then He either had to walk to these places over the period of his forty-day fast, or He was supernaturally transported there.

There is another possibility.

In the biblical book of Hebrews, the writer discusses the appearance of The Seed and how he interacts with the time-space world. There is much that could be said about this, but I want to focus only on this statement about Jesus: He was tempted *just as we are*, yet without sin.[5] And how are we tempted? It's a battle of the mind. We'll talk more about that battle later, but in this context we want to make the point that Jesus' encounter with the rebel elohim needn't have been with a physical manifestation of him. If The Seed experienced temptation as we do, then it is likely that, in His weakened state of hunger, His mind and will were targeted by the most cunning rebel in history. Imagine how vulnerable a starving man would be to delusion, or in this case, imagine how easy it might be for a shrewd enemy to manipulate, tempt and deceive someone in a state of near starvation.

That The Seed would be alert enough to recognize the ruse is an indication of His essentially spiritual nature. That alertness is displayed again later in His time-space visit when a friend tries to convince him to abandon His purpose. The friend was His follower, Peter, but Jesus instantly perceived that the deceiver was, once again, manipulating, not in tangible form, but behind the scenes. Imagine Peter's surprise when Jesus reacts to him by saying, "Get away from me, Satan!" Jesus didn't need to be able to see a fallen angel to know that his influence was present. [6]

In short, Jesus' encounter with the devil didn't need to be physical to make it Biblical. It is easy for us to imagine the encounter with a real "person" but, based on our personal experience, we can just as easily imagine the inner conflict that we know as temptation. I think that's exactly how the temptation of The Seed played out.

---

[5] Hebrews 4:15
[6] Matthew 16:23; Mark 8:33.

The second apparent reference to the physical presence of a fallen angel in time dimension is when Paul the Apostle warns, "Satan disguises himself as an angel of light."[7] But the apostle uses that terminology as a caution against humans who are behaving outside of submission as Satan was. In fact, earlier in the same chapter, Paul mentions how the serpent deceived Eve in the garden...and we know how that turned out for "Snake," the rebel commander. Still, Paul's reference to that angelic ability isn't proof of that ability operating presently.

The idea that rebel elohim no longer manifest physically isn't any more conjectural than the idea that they do. The accounts of submitted angels taking on physical form are all over the biblical narrative; we are even told that we might encounter them without knowing it,[8] but the evidence that fallen angels behave similarly is scarce and not beyond doubt. Personally, I am relieved that I don't have to worry that the stranger sitting next to me on the bus is a demon in tangible form. I have enough problems dealing with the fear and deception that are the main weapons at the disposal of the disembodied rebels.

The presence of rebel elohim in physical form is conspicuous by its absence after the days of Noah. We have to wonder if the Creator didn't put a guard on the passageway between the dimensions as he had earlier, only this time on the eternal side of the boundary. Furthermore, there is an enigmatic comment made by Peter, one of Jesus' inner circle, that may shed some light on the subject. Let's jump ahead a few thousand years and read what Peter wrote.

> For Christ also died for sins once for all, the just for the unjust, so that He might bring us to God, having been put to death in the flesh, but made alive in the spirit; in which also He went and *made proclamation to the spirits now in prison, who once were disobedient*, when the patience of God kept waiting in the days of Noah, during the construction of the

---

[7] 2 Corinthians 11:14.

[8] Hebrews 13:2.

ark, in which a few, that is, eight persons, were brought safely through the water.[9]

Peter was encouraging the followers of Jesus Christ to live their lives in obedience and submission to the Creator. As he does, he makes reference to the incident back in Noah's day. There is a phrase to which I've added emphasis. Jesus—aka, "The Seed"—made a proclamation to some spirits, some *disobedient* spirits. Some say that those disobedient spirits were really humans who had died and needed to hear the message of the gospel that Jesus was preaching. There are some reasons that doesn't work, including that the word *proclamation* has the sense of an official announcement or decree [10] as opposed to some sort of evangelistic message. So what else could Peter be hinting at? Could the spirits he is referring to be elohim and the decree a statement of their imprisonment, something like house arrest? I think it's likely. Not only does it fit the timing of the conspicuous disappearance of disobedient elohim in the time/space dimension, but the word translated "prison" has a strong connotation of a person being placed under guard. The suggestion is that the rebels were to be limited until some future time when their case was to be decided once and for all.

And there are other reasons to draw that conclusion. Early in Jesus' ministry, when he encounters some of the rebel elohim inhabiting a man, the spirits (the Bible calls them demons) yell out, "Why are you bothering us, Son of God? You have no right to torture us before God's appointed time!" Interesting. They not only knew who He was, as though they had encountered Him before, but they knew their time was running out. Later, Jesus, referring to the perils of living selfishly, mentions that there is a place prepared for such

---

[9] 1 Peter 3:18-20 (NAS).

[10] Elsewhere in the Bible we learn that for those born into time, they don't get another chance in the eternal realm to make it right. One shot is all anybody gets. That doesn't fit with this interpretation of what Peter is saying.

miscreants (the Bible describes the place as being always on fire).[11]

Elsewhere, Peter, the disciple, remarks that, "God did not spare even the angels when they sinned; he threw them into hell, in gloomy caves and darkness until the judgment day." [12] The word translated 'hell' needs some attention. It might better be translated, "he placed them under restraint." The original Greek word is Tartarus and it is a word that is only used in this instance in all the New Testament. According to Greek and Roman mythology Tartarus is the dark, gloomy place where the Titans, a race of powerful "deities," were chained up—picture a prison. Finally, in the little New Testament book of Jude it says in verse 6,

> And I remind you of the angels who did not stay within the limits of authority God gave them but left the place where they belonged. God has kept them chained in prisons of darkness, waiting for the Day of Judgment.

So the question is, what kind of prison are the rebels in? There are two things that appear to have happened to the rebel army. First, as I described above, they were banned from directly entering the physical world. They are active in the physical world, but not in any material sense. Second, they were expelled from the presence of the Creator and from among the obedient eternal beings.

They became a race without a world to live in, trapped between eternity and space.

In essence, the imprisonment amounted to becoming disembodied vagrant ghosts. Here is how Jesus (The Seed) describes the plight of what he calls "an unclean spirit." He pictures such a creature when unattached to a human as being like a person (maybe a defeated soldier) wandering in the desert, looking for a well from which to drink.[13] In the

---

[11] Matthew 25:41.

[12] 2 Peter 2:4.

[13] Matthew 12:43 and Luke 11:24.

analogy, we humans are the wells. Perhaps a more graphic comparison might be a parasite detached from its host. Later, in a place called Gadera, Jesus commands rebel elohim to leave a human host.[14] Interestingly, the demons beg The Seed to let them enter the bodies of some local pigs rather than, as Jesus described, wander in the desert. So, on the time/space side of things, the elohim are stripped of their amphibious qualities. They can no longer visit the time/space dimension in physical form.

On the eternal side of things, the rebel elohim have suffered an even more humiliating defeat. The record of it appears in the very last book of the Bible, the book of Revelation. In the twelfth chapter an account of a fierce battle in the eternal dimension is recorded.

> Then there was war in heaven. Michael and the angels under his command fought the dragon and his angels. And the dragon lost the battle and was forced out of heaven. This great dragon—the ancient serpent called the Devil, or Satan, the one deceiving the whole world—was thrown down to the earth with all his angels. Then I heard a loud voice shouting across the heavens, "It has happened at last—the salvation and power and kingdom of our God, and the authority of his Christ! For the Accuser has been thrown down to earth—the one who accused our brothers and sisters before our God day and night. And they have defeated him because of the blood of the Lamb and because of their testimony. And they were not afraid to die. Rejoice, O heavens! And you who live in the heavens, rejoice! But terror will come on the earth and the sea. For the Devil has come down to you in great anger, and he knows that he has little time."[15]

It should be said that there are many suggestions about the exact timing of this event. Some scholars suggest that the expulsion of the rebels from heaven is a future event, part of the timetable of the last days of history. My objection to that

---

[14] Matthew chapter 8.
[15] Revelation 12:7-12.

interpretation is that I am not convinced that we can make a one-to-one correlation between time in our dimension, and "time," if there is such a thing, in the eternal dimension where the events in Revelation 12 occurred. Personally, I think this war took place in the days of Noah and that it is a response to the declaration brought to the heavenly places when The Seed appeared, quite unexpectedly, before the rebel armies.

The Clash of the Eternal Ones

It may have happened this way. Roll the tape.

The scene opens through an enormous portal looking into the time/space dimension and down on the earth. A blinding flash of lightning splits the angry, dark clouds below followed by a jaw-rattling crack of thunder. Somewhere beneath the clouds there is the sound of a heavy wooden door closing, then the sound of rain. It builds to a deafening roar. The water is rising. There is screaming—desperate human voices. Countless people are dying. The sound reaches a crescendo and then diminishes until only the rain can be heard.

The great cleansing has begun.

The camera pulls back into the eternals and the angle widens to take in the whole portal. Through it can be seen the arc of the time/space earth, cloaked in steel-grey clouds. Suddenly, there is a sound like the flapping of a million frightened bats. The rebel elohim pour through the portal back into their native dimension. As they do, the camera angle widens still more until the whole retreating army is in view, framed against the open window into time/space.

The camera pans 180 degrees to reveal what lies behind. A vast army of the elohim who remain loyal to the Creator is massed and ready to engage the retreating rebels who are hemmed between them and the door.

Suddenly a figure appears at the portal. He glows with brilliant light and carries a sword that pulses with some kind of luminous energy. He has one foot in the heavenly dimension and one foot in time/space and seems equally prepared to be in either.

It is the last person the rebels expect to encounter here. From their limited understanding of time, The Seed wasn't supposed to even exist until some human woman gave birth to Him, yet here He is. They had underestimated the power of the Creator again, not knowing that He had made a place for Himself in the time/space world at the moment He had created it. He had created the earth from the inside out.

The voice of The Seed roars across the eternal sky. "Hear this, disobedient spirits! You are banished! The door into the world of the time-creatures is closed to you…" Two fearsome angels—cherubim—come forward to guard the gateway.

The rebel commander, arrogant even in defeat, steps brazenly forward and addresses The Seed. "I have a right to the time-creatures. I won them. You gave the time/space dimension to them and they gave it to me. You can't keep me out of what is mine!"

The Seed responds: "You still have access. I only bar you from space; I am not keeping you out of time. Time is your prison. That will be the battlefield on which you will be defeated by the very ones you thought you could control. Mark my words. The time-creatures will choose to be mine again. Your claim on them shall be nullified when they have submitted to Me. They will be restored and you will be destroyed. Furthermore, your presence among the holy angels is forbidden."

One of the elohim known as Michael steps forward from among the loyalists. The Snake steps forward to meet him. The clash of the eternal ones begins.

At battle's end the rebel elohim have been defeated, driven back from the eternal dimension into a murky region not fully heaven and not fully earth. From it they will be able interact with the beings in the time/space but not enter their dimension. The rebel elohim now roam in what amounts to a second heaven outside of space, forcing a change in strategy.

Cage Match

From the earthbound perspective these elohim have been condemned to inhabit an invisible world, a world of spirit. It is foreign to them and to the time-creatures.

The time-creatures are a part of it because they have a spiritual side to their nature, yet this second heaven, if we can call it that, is foreign to them because it exists outside of all that they can touch, feel and smell. They have an instinctive knowledge that something lays beyond their senses; a vestige of the part of them that was designed to be connected to the eternal, the part of human nature that went dormant when the first time-creatures rejected the Creator's design. But without an energized spirit life, they can only connect to that spiritual world at the level of mind, emotions and what might be called instinct or spiritual intuition.

The second heaven is also foreign to the defeated elohim because it is outside of eternity, their native dimension, just as it is outside of space, the realm of the humans. Created for the eternal dimension, the fallen ones suddenly find themselves confined by time—the ticking clock marks their dwindling freedom. It is as though the rebel elohim suddenly find that they are wearing a stopwatch around their neck. Until now it has not been possible to say of an angel that time is running out.

In this new configuration, the nature of the combat between angelic and human beings becomes clearly defined. In Roman times, gladiators would fight to the death in horrific spectacles where the combatants would face each other in a locked arena. Before thousands of onlookers the fighters would duel to the death. The closest parallel we have might be an event known as the cage-match in "Pro Wrestling," or *The Hunger Games*, in Suzanne Collins' novel of the same name. In the first, the "wrestlers" are locked in a chain-link cage so that neither contestant can leave the ring, either by choice or by being hurled out by his opponent. The idea is that the contestants beat one another senseless until only one is left standing. In

57

Collins' grim, post apocalyptic tale, there is a hi-tech cage match in which 24 randomly selected teens are confined in an arena where they do battle until only one remains alive.

You may have already figured out that the caged elohim are what the Bible calls "demons." Genesis marks the downward spiral of a fraction of the race of eternal-ones who, because of rebellion become destined to eternal destruction. Consider that thought for a moment. I didn't say simply "destruction" as though these beings were going to be dismantled molecule by molecule and blasted into nothingness, but *eternal destruction*, that is a never-ending process. The concept is hard to wrap our minds around, but the fact is, when a being is created eternal—outside of time—then it is going to live forever. That is true of time-creatures, too. They were created to be native to time/space but they were destined to have access to eternity. So the issue isn't if the created races are going to exist forever, the issue is *where* they will exist; in what relation to the rest of creation.

So, picture the defeated elohim army locked in a "time-cage" with the humans. Here two races will fight to the death. One race is doomed to face the consequences of its decision, made in eternity, to live as rebels. The other, having been born in time and space has the option of again yielding its will to the Creator, who is the source of unlimited power, and regaining its destiny.

So, what is the destiny to which the time-creatures are to return? The ancient writings aren't specific about what lay ahead for creation if it had remained fully synchronized with the original specifications of the Creator. Apparently we're on a "need to know" basis about that and we don't need to know yet. But this much we know, eventually the Creator intends to bring everything back to the point where that destiny will be open to us. The guards at the door into eternity will be ordered to stand down and humans, those who have learned how to be fully submitted, will be free to walk in the eternal dimension, at last living in the fullness of their capability. Furthermore, we will be introduced to that other race of created beings, the ones who have remained submitted from the beginning to the Creator and his creation. The ancient writings contain many descriptions of encounters between them and the time-creatures, but those meetings are anything but routine. One day they will be. In the meantime, creation on both sides of the boundary is waiting. The Apostle Paul describes it:

> For the creation was subjected to futility, not willingly, but because of Him who subjected it, in hope that the creation itself also will be set free from its slavery to corruption into the freedom of the glory of the children of God. For we know that *the whole creation groans and suffers the pains of childbirth together until now. And not only this, but also we ourselves, having the first fruits of the Spirit, even we ourselves groan within ourselves, waiting eagerly for our adoption as sons*, the redemption of our body. For in hope we have been saved, but hope that is seen is not hope; for who hopes for what he already sees? But if we hope for what we do not see, with perseverance we wait eagerly for it.[16]

What will it be like when, someday, we time-creatures meet, "hand to hand" as it were, that part of creation we call angels, both created races coexisting? The New Testament describes it this way: "you have come to Mount Zion, to the city of the living God, the heavenly Jerusalem, and to thousands of angels in joyful assembly."[17]

All of this has something to do with The Seed. To the dismay of the rebels He wasn't a creature of time and space; in fact He wasn't something created at all, rather He was the presence of the Creator himself, as much of Him as could be contained in the limitations of whatever dimension He was in. Yet, the Creator's words in the third chapter of Genesis still stand: The Seed—the seed of woman—is going to be born into time/space as though He were nothing more than a time-creature. During the days of Noah, that part of the story had

---

[16] Romans 8:20-25 (NLT). Italics mine.
[17] Hebrews 12:22.

yet to be told, but the whole narrative of what we call the Bible is the telling of it; the story of The Seed and how he makes it possible for the time-creatures to recover their destiny, and what it means for them to submit to the Creator and attain the potential that He originally designed for them.

Change of Strategy

After the days of Noah, the strategy of the rebels changed again out of necessity. With each new raid on the time-creatures they learned something new about their own limitations and about the weapons that remained available to them. Unfortunately for them, they passed the point of no return the instant they chose disobedience instead of submission. After the clash in Noah's time, their best hope became to take as many time creatures down with them as they could before the end.

To summarize, the first enemy assault was on the "spirit interface" of the time-creatures. The results of that attack were substantial, but not irreversible. The second attack was on the human genetic code, an attempt to bring corruption into the human line. The impact was horrific; it required the destruction of virtually the entire race of time-creatures. But again, the Creator countered the enemy thrust. Now, the only vulnerability left in the race of time-creatures is what is called the soul—mind and emotions and will.

The human soul is detached from the Creator. To compensate, the time-creatures have come to rely on their senses—their body—being scarcely aware that while they are busy with the tangible world the spiritual part of their nature is vulnerable to attack. Let's skip ahead a few chapters in Genesis and see what we can learn about the nature of this new warfare. As we do, one thing will become clear. The time-creatures will have to wake up and discover what weapons are available to them for self-defense and for counter attack.

This is the cage-match of Genesis 6. As it plays out, the key to the victory will be learning submission.

Chapter 4

Mission Not So Impossible

Imagine the fun you could have if you were invisible. The shoelaces you could tie together! The doors you could slam when nobody was looking! The things you could whisper into a person's ear without them knowing who said it. What fun!

Now imagine the damage that an invisible army could do.

That is a pretty accurate description of the nature of the struggle between heaven and earth today. Trapped in a spiritual prison, the rebel elohim have access only to the soulish part of human beings.[1] But being trapped doesn't mean that they are powerless. On the contrary, stealth and deception are potent weapons in the hands of an army that functions invisibly. Furthermore, the time-creatures (that includes us) are largely ignorant of the composition of the created universe and therefore become dupes, not knowing that they have a spiritual side to their nature that is vulnerable to attack from what the New Testament calls "heavenly places." The rebels are skilled at invisibly manipulating human minds, emotions, and intuitive sense, with the result that time-creatures can be hindered physically, deceived into collaboration with the enemy, and in some cases, lured into willing cooperation.

---

[1] Some would object that demons can also inflict physical harm on people. We don't disagree, but would suggest that such physical harm by fallen angels does not emanate from outside of the individual, unless at the hands of another person. Rather, demons compromise the body by manipulating the psychic nature of a person resulting in the deterioration and sometimes enhancement of the body. See Merrill F. Unger, Demons in the World Today. Tyndale, 1988.

Fallen Motives

But what's in it for the elohim? By now, you'd think that they would know they were beaten. What possible reason could they have to use and abuse the time-creatures and continue this hopeless struggle against the Creator?

Illogical though it may seem, unfulfilled selfishness often deteriorates into utter cruelty. We see it in human nature. When someone who is motivated by selfishness is denied his self-serving goal, he often acts to prevent others from achieving their goals. This is what inflames a spurned lover to kill the woman he supposedly loves— "If I can't have her, nobody can have her." It is what provokes someone who feels like a failure to randomly shoot those who he judges to be successful. Irrational vindictiveness is not uncommon in the world. And what would we expect? If the rebels are practiced manipulators of human souls why wouldn't humans begin to reflect the same irrational hatreds and embrace the same self-serving objectives as their enemy?

Now, this isn't to say that men and women are absolved from responsibility for disobedience. "The will," that pesky part of human nature, can be as much a problem for us as it is for any of the creatures God made, either human or angelic. It's just that an invisible enemy that can target the mechanism by which we make our choices (mind, emotions, and intuitive senses) can influence us to wrongly activate our will so that we choose poorly. We can choose poorly without outside help, but a little malicious nudge from an invisible enemy can make things much worse.

Our next stop in Genesis is chapter 11, but before we get there let's summarize where we've been and what happens after the flood. So far, we've touched down in two chapters, Genesis 3, where the human spirit becomes detached from the Creator; and Genesis 6, where the human race is wiped out because of a corrupt partnership between human and elohim. This is when the rebels are imprisoned. The next few chapters discuss Noah's seafaring adventure, the nature of the relationships within his family (including an incident that seems to have the fingerprints of covert elohim all over it), and a description of the agreement that the Creator makes with this "second creation." Included in that agreement is the instruction at the beginning of the 9th chapter: be fruitful and multiply and fill the earth. This is important. It amounts to a "to-do list" for this fresh crop of time-creatures.

Then, in chapter 10 there is a genealogy of Noah's descendents. I want to zero in on one parenthetical portion in that.

> Now Cush became the father of Nimrod; he became a mighty one on the earth. He was a mighty hunter before the LORD; therefore it is said, "Like Nimrod a mighty hunter before the LORD." The beginning of his kingdom was Babel and Erech and Accad and Calneh, in the land of Shinar. From that land he went forth into Assyria, and built Nineveh and Rehoboth-Ir and Calah, and Resen between Nineveh and Calah; that is the great city.[2]

Nimrod is singled out as a kingdom builder and a wielder of power. He is described as a "mighty hunter" and a "mighty one." Historically, he is credited with being the first effective ruler of the vast territories that later evolve into the Assyrian and Babylonian empires. To this day, there are sites in the region of ancient Mesopotamia that bear his name. Moreover, Nimrod was a conqueror and a despot who consolidated his power and subjugated significant populations in the region. With the power of numbers and the weapon of invasive force this early warlord personifies willful disobedience. It is on his watch that Chapter 11 begins.

All for One

Based on what you know about the nature of the war in the heavenly places, what, or who, do you think might be behind the figurehead we know as Nimrod? Also, based on what you

---

[2] Genesis 10:8 (NASB).

know about the new strategies of war in the heavenly places, is it any surprise what happens next among the time-creatures:

> At one time the whole world spoke a single language and used the same words. As the people migrated eastward, they found a plain in the land of Babylonia and settled there. They began to talk about construction projects. "Come," they said, "let's make great piles of burnt brick and collect natural asphalt to use as mortar. Let's build a great city with a tower that reaches to the skies—a monument to our greatness! This will bring us together and keep us from scattering all over the world." [3]

Notice a couple of things. First, note what these time-creatures are trying to avoid: scattering. Rather than submit to God's instructions about being fruitful and filling the earth, these people want to stick together. Not only that, they want to make a name for themselves, climb the ladder of power and fame. Finally, they want to achieve heaven on their own terms. Their construction projects were religious monuments, something like towers. These are three things that stand in opposition to the Creator's blueprint: disobedience, idol worship, and self-aggrandizement.

If you can picture puppets on a string, you can probably imagine what is going on in the heavenly places. You can visualize strings attached to these time-creatures, tugging on their spiritual senses, tangling their emotions, and wrapping around their minds. The deceptions behind disobedience, idolatry and pride, aren't much different than the first ancient lies. Remember? Eve was conned into believing that she needed more than she had; that she would be like her Creator in even more significant ways than she was already, and that she could accomplish those things by her own effort. The distance between picking some forbidden fruit and building a tower of worship isn't as far as we might imagine.

---

[3] Genesis 11:1-4 (NLT).

But there is something more going on here. It has to do with the power of unity. The central issue isn't just that everybody spoke the same language, it is that speaking the same language made them one; a powerful unit working toward a single goal. The matter is important enough for the Creator to once again step onto the stage of history and deliver one of those speeches.

> The LORD came down to see the city and the tower which the sons of men had built. The LORD said, "Behold, they are one people, and they all have the same language. And this is what they began to do, and now *nothing which they purpose to do will be impossible for them*. Come, let Us go down and there confuse their language, so that they will not understand one another's speech." So the LORD scattered them abroad from there over the face of the whole earth; and they stopped building the city.[4]

I have quoted from the New American Standard Bible because that translation better conveys the phrase I've italicized: *Nothing will be impossible for them...* Notice that the Creator is observing the work of *unsubmitted people*. The suggestion here is that there is vast, inherent power when time-creatures function with a single purpose. These time-creatures are operating in disobedience yet the Creator, Himself assesses the potential of their joint efforts as limitless. Covertly, the elohim are attempting to seize and manipulate the last source of eternal power that remains available to them, unity. If successful, they will effectively forge the mass of individual time-creatures into a single functioning unit. That isn't a bad thing, theoretically. Apparently, part of the Creator's design is for there to be a community functioning as one. The problem is that such a powerful unit in the wrong hands could upset the balance of creation. That's why the Creator intervenes a third time and adjusts the interface between the eternal and the time/space dimensions.

---

[4] Genesis 11:5-8 (NAS).

In the garden, the Creator limited the exchange between the dimensions by placing the interface under guard from the time/space side. He did the same thing in the days of Noah; that time from the infinite/eternal side. Now, in Genesis 11, the Creator puts a hold on yet another component of creation; the power of cooperation and unity. Such power must only be exercised from a place of submission. The full expression of this capability will also have to wait for The Seed.

Much later, in John's gospel, we learn that The Seed (Jesus) is to be executed, crucified. Then we are told—keep in mind what happened in Nimrod's day—that one of the results of Jesus' death would be, "for the gathering together of all the children of God scattered around the world." A short time later, foreigners, like the "passengers" coming to the ark in Noah's day, begin to come to Jesus. Then, Jesus calls his followers to oneness. After His execution and subsequent resurrection, this unified group experiences the evidence of a reconnected spirit, and demonstrates an ability to overcome the barrier of language.[5]

Isn't that interesting? The outcome of The Seed's presence in time/space repeals the estrangement of Eden, empowers the time-creatures for effective defense against the demonic consequences of the days of Noah, and reverses the scattering of Babel.

Preparation and Re-education

At last, the battle lines are drawn. The playing field has been leveled. The time-race is temporarily stripped of access to the eternal realm and prohibited from experiencing the power of union. The elohim are barred from the spatial world and confined to a region that has only one thing left in common with the earthly dimension, time. The two races are now locked in battle. The outcome will mean the ultimate destruction of all of the rebel elohim and a significant number

---

[5] John 11:52; 12:20-21; 13:34-35; 17:11,21,22; Acts 2:1-12.

of the time-creatures who embrace their rebellion; but most excitingly, it will result in the bringing together of all things in heaven and on earth[6] a condition that has not been seen since the rebellion in the garden.

From our perspective on this side of the dimensional boundary, the weapons of this war are spiritual. The key weapons in the elohim arsenal are invisibility, deception and fear; in ours, they are knowledge and submission.

The time-creatures will need knowledge in order to engage the rebel elohim, and to recognize the coming of The Seed through whom The Plan will be accomplished. They are a clear target without such understanding. They need to know the nature of their enemy and the character of their Creator, otherwise they will not have the resources they need to operate their will, that part of their nature that can return them to their destiny. Without an informed will, we time-creatures won't know enough to choose to submit to the Creator and The Plan he designed. We need clear understanding if we are to grasp the source of strength, and be able to choose wisely.

Fortunately, the Creator has been placing those markers in history for that purpose. They are about to become very important.

Up to now, the story has been about the elohim and the rebellion that took place among them, and about the time-creatures, all of them, the whole race. But now that the battlefield has been established, the Creator begins an intense program of re-education for the humans. The centerpiece of that program is a man named Abram, soon to be "Abraham." He represents a single lineage through which the Creator intends to reveal the benefits of submission and the consequences of disobedience. This family line will be the messenger of the Creator. It will carry many of those markers—symbols.

Why Abraham? Why his descendents, the ones that will come to be known as "the Jews." Well, why not? Truthfully,

---

[6] Ephesians 3:10.

the Creator could have singled out any group for this purpose, but he settled on Abraham. We may never know if there were others among the time-creatures that were willing to submit, who exercised that important quality of trust. What we do know is that Abraham believed his Creator and submitted himself. The rest, as they say, is history.

Abraham's family becomes the case study of a relationship with the Creator. The children of Abraham have been singled out. Sometimes they will be a good example of walking in concert with Him, other times they will be poster children for rebellion and failure. All the while, their history is recorded for the instruction of future generations.

This single ethnic unit has become central in the unfolding story of The Seed that the Creator mentioned in Eden. The story of Abraham's offspring serves three purposes.

First, as I just mentioned, they were to be a case study on obedience. As such, they would reveal much about the character of the Creator, and even more about human nature. What we learn about submission from the children of Abraham is vital as we prepare to re-enter a relationship with the Creator and regain our capacity to enter the eternal dimension.

Second, Israel would provide the historical and prophetic signposts—those markers—that would identify the Creator's strategy for reversing the rebellion in the garden. For millennia after Eden, what the Creator called "The Seed" was, in a manner of speaking, waiting in the wings. Based on what we learn from the first encounter with the Creator in Genesis, we discovered that whoever this person was to be, he was going to strike a decisive blow against the elohim commander, and secure the ultimate defeat of the rebellion in the eternal realm. Moreover, The Seed was to be born from the race of the time-creatures. Just when He was to be born and how we were to recognize Him was not clear. The descendents of Abraham would clarify those things through their prophetic writings and religious traditions. The spiritual life of the Jews was to be strewn with symbols that anticipated the story of The Seed.

Finally, Israel would be the delivery system for The Seed Himself. The Seed would be born from a genetically uniform race—an ethnic microcosm—in order to restore a spiritually unified race.

For that to happen, though, the time-creatures would, one by one, have to make the same decision that the first time-creatures made so poorly. They would have to make the decision to submit to the Creator's intended design, to agree with Him in heart and practice. But deciding to submit—believing the Creator—is only the first step. The learned practices of a fallen race have to be unlearned by this new and emerging race. A new way of life, consistent with The Plan of the Creator has to be adopted.

Un-learning

I heard a story of a young man with a promising career ahead of him in the chemical industry. As he sat at his desk, an explosion in the nearby loading area shattered a window. It also shattered his world. As fragments of glass filled the air, his eyesight, like a candle in a windstorm, flickered out and he was plunged into utter darkness.

In the days that followed his sudden blindness, all that had been familiar became strange. When friends came to visit, he could no longer see their face, but had to identify them by their voice. Finding his way around the house required him to touch the walls as he walked, or to reach for familiar features with his hands. This new life was a struggle, and there were moments that he wanted to give up hope, but gradually his sense of touch became more acute, his hearing more sensitive—he began to probe the darkness with his remaining senses.

Most of us have known of people who have grappled with limitations and compensated for them in ways that have astonished and inspired us: The woman without arms that has developed remarkable dexterity in her feet; or the hearing impaired man who can feel faint vibrations. Such cases testify to the amazing ability of the human brain. It is doubtful, however, that any with a physical disability would not prefer to be fully functional. Given the option, the young man in the story would certainly choose to see.

Adam and Eve's experience was similar to that of the young man, though more catastrophic. Playing too near that tree—the one that had to do with knowledge of good and evil—was the spiritual equivalent of playing with dynamite. The resulting explosion cost them their spiritual eyes and ears—what the Bible calls their "spirit." Not that they didn't have one any more, only it didn't work like it once did.

By that act of *"tree-sin"* they made the conscious decision to rebel and abandon submission to their Creator. They lost the right to live as citizens of the unified creation of heaven and earth—worse, they lost the *ability*. Suddenly, they were unable to perceive beyond the world of sight and sound. With their spirit disconnected and no longer in command of their lives, there was no way to follow orders from the throne of the Creator. They were forced to make do with what senses they had left: eyes, ears, and hands; mind, emotions, and intuition—spirit off-line, soul and body leading the way.

That was the condition that was passed down through the corrupted DNA of our original parents. Where there had once been open access to the Creator's presence, humanity was suddenly isolated from Him. Where His will had been clear and His purposes evident there was silence. The Creator (God) had given them the choice of being subject to his loving presence. They had chosen independence.

Happily, that wasn't the end of the story. God is a God of choices, and though His human creations are prone to choose poorly, He was faithful to start paving the road back. For that purpose He used a single family, a man called Abraham and his descendants, Isaac and Israel. From among these descendents came prophets, people with a God-initiated role and unusually keen spiritual insight. They came to remind Israel and, by extension, the rest of the time-creatures, of their options. Ultimately, in God's most eloquent appeal, he offered to open the door to an Eden-like relationship with him through The Seed, who, when He was born into time/space was to be called, Jesus. The first Adam had been under subjection to God, but chose independence…and blindness. Then Jesus, who is called "the second Adam," offers a restored relationship with God to the time-creatures, the opportunity to see again. If we take Him up on His offer, we can learn how to follow in the way it was originally intended. Learning to follow is what submission is all about.

And here is where we get into trouble. This business of submission has been so skewed in our understanding that it has become repugnant to us. If you think about it, that should come as no surprise. Remember we are at war. There is an invisible army that, ever since Genesis, has been all about control and taking over. Even after God placed severe sanctions over that band of rebels, they continue to launch assaults on the human soul. Nimrod, the despot and tyrant, was the classic example of how an attack of that kind looks from the time/space side of things. And to this day, we tend to see submission in terms of control and domination. But that isn't it at all. Real submission, the kind that comes from being in sync with The Plan, isn't about keeping order or determining who is in charge. Submission isn't an end in itself, it is a restored way of life that is necessary if we time-creatures are to be reintegrated with the realm of the eternal.

On Being "Bi-Lingual"

For the natives this side of eternity (that would be us), it is about choosing to see and hear again, and about relearning what might be called the language of Eden.

A European friend of mine once asked, "Do you know what someone who can speak two languages is called?"

I had a sense I was being set up. "Bi-lingual…" I answered, cautiously.

"Correct," he said. "How about, three languages?"

I was waiting for the hammer to fall, but I answered again: "Tri-lingual?"

He smiled. "Right, again. Do you know what they call someone who speaks only one language?"

I hesitated for a moment. Just long enough for him to answer his own question.

"An *American*!" he said, and burst into laughter.

Sadly, he is right. Americans are well known for speaking only English—some of us don't even speak that very well. The reason is partially laid to the fact that we are fairly isolated geographically from other language groups. We haven't really needed to know anything but English. More than that, there is a stubborn resistance among Americans to learning other languages.

A befuddled American tourist in Mexico had to ask a local villager for directions. The traveler knew enough Spanish to understand basic directions, and say thank you, but she had the feeling the she needed to know what, "*No, debe,*" and something about "*la agua,*" followed by something else she didn't quite understand, meant. Back at the hotel, after a hot day of sightseeing, she looked up the words in her English/Spanish dictionary. Unfortunately, the translation, having to do with drinking dirty water, came too late for her to avoid an evening of Montezuma's revenge—a very American case of diarrhea. How she wished she better understood Spanish!

The human soul was once bi-lingual. It understood the language of the spirit—both the human spirit and the Spirit of God. But without that ability, the soul began to make its own way, functioning independently of the spirit, unwilling and unable to respond to its direction. The activity of the independent soul is impulsive, taking its cues from the rebels who are taking potshots from the heavenly places. What we call lust, pride and sensuality are often "hits" we've taken from there. Our soul tends to ignore the warnings of the spirit about this stuff because it prefers it's own language to the language of eternity, which it has all but forgotten.

This is perhaps the most significant way that the image of God in human beings has been marred. Scripturally, God is revealed as being triune in nature. The term, "triune" is not a biblical one, but it is useful to describe the Creator in terms that are understandable.

What it describes is a multifaceted being who exists outside of all we know as "creation." But, God also is fully present within it. He exists in the eternal dimension, what we call "heaven," and in time/space, what we call earth or "the world." The terms Holy Spirit, Father, and Son, are an attempt to explain his presence in the whole of creation. There are not three gods, one for each dimension, but one God constantly modeling for us the twin relationships of communion and communication. As God is, so we are in our capacity for relating to Him.

Scholar, philosopher, and Christian apologist, Francis Schaeffer, declared, "I would still be an agnostic if there were no Trinity, because there would be no answers..."[7] Shaeffer understood that the different facets of God's nature, Father, Son, and Holy Spirit— "three persons in existence, loving each other, and in communication with each other, before all else was"—were reflected in the three-pronged nature of people. Spirit, soul, and body were to interrelate in a way similar to the relationship within God's nature. If that internal interaction is interrupted (as it was in Eden) a vital element of human nature is missing.

God designed Adam and Eve to live in submission to His headship. He designed us to commune with Him, His Spirit with ours. The result of that Spirit-to-spirit communication was a soul in proper subjection to the will of God, and the body, in turn, lovingly restrained and cared for. This relationship was supposed to be at work in each of us, our

---

[7] Francis Schaeffer, *He is There and He is Not Silent*, Wheaton: Tyndale House, 1972, p. 14, 15.

physical wants and our emotional tendencies coming under the authority of our spiritual nature, which, if everything is wired properly, is supposed to be responding to the Spirit of our Creator. But, fallen human life (for that is what life without an energized spirit is) wobbles along like an unbalanced washing machine during spin cycle—the soul, resisting the knowledge of God and throwing our lives, first one way, then the other, with no influence to stabilize its wild gyrations.

This is definitely not what God had in mind. He intended his human creations to be working in compliance with His will. As long as they did that, there was no reason He couldn't count on them to, "be fruitful and multiply, fill the whole earth and *subdue it*." In this word, subdue, there is a hint of the importance of submission. God gave human beings a significant responsibility: Get behind the wheel and drive this creation.

Cosmic Driving

On a slightly less cosmic scale, I have an idea of what that means. I was the nervous parent of an aspiring teen driver. A friend of ours told us that his experience with his own teen driver was one of the most frightening of his life. His admission wouldn't have worried me except he was a helicopter pilot who had flown rescue missions in the Persian Gulf! Apparently, flying low to the ground and dodging missiles was restful compared to driving with his adolescent daughter.

Our concern was our son, Caleb, age 13. He has a significantly different approach to life than we do. As parents, we are steadfast, stable, think-twice kind of people. We ponder and plan; reflect and ruminate. Caleb, by contrast, learns by doing. When we are driving along as a family and he asks how fast the car will go with the "pedal to the metal" we know that our simple answer to the question probably won't be enough. We know that he very much wants to test our answer on the open road.

Making a responsible driver out of an impulsive, inexperienced teen takes time and training. To "fill the whole earth and subdue it" takes training, too. That was the lesson our first parents failed to learn. They needed to be under authority in order to have authority, just as we do. Falling short of that, they were ejected from God's presence, and came under subjection to the very creation they were to have governed, and into bondage to their own disobedience, what we have come to call 'sin.'

In the film, *Forrest Gump,* my generation was personified as the hapless simpleton played by Tom Hanks in the title role. During the '60s baby boomers in my age bracket naïvely perfected a popular sense of estrangement that has since evolved into bitter nihilism. Social commentators have suggested that the root of rebellion in those days was disillusionment with society and culture. Perhaps. But I suspect it goes deeper. The music of the period decried a sense of lostness and declared a yearning to get back to something; to rediscover innocence; to get back to the garden.

The ancient writings of the Bible point the way back to Eden, not the literal return to a place, but a returning of heart to the relationship that existed there. The Creator (God) began paving the road back to wholeness (human life, ruled by the human spirit rightly submitted to the Spirit of God) almost from the very instant that the relationship between the first time-creatures and their Creator was broken.

The Genesis story sets the stage for the great restoration. The first eleven chapters describe how the war that broke out in the eternal dimension came to be fought in time/space. The part of the Bible we call the Old Testament paves the road back. Every step and misstep among the descendants of Abraham, Isaac and Israel, are a lesson about submission. Prophecy after prophecy points to the coming of The Seed, God's secret weapon for reviving a once dead race. We know him as Jesus. His death and resurrection healed the damage to the human spirit done in the garden.

What's more, His life became the prototype for that new, restored race. His actions, His example, and the things He taught became the template for it. He is the living training manual. Until He came, the broken time-race could only yearn for intimacy with its Creator God. Now, one by one, members of that race can choose to submit to Him, and then begin the process of relearning what it means to be a citizen of both earth and heaven.

Chapter 5

Who's Holding the Rope?

In the previous chapters we have been exploring the history of creation, spending nearly all of our time in the years that preceded Abraham and his son Isaac, and Isaac's son Jacob, the one who came to be called Israel. All of that (the Old Testament in the Bible) was preparatory to the coming of The Seed, which is the subject of the part of the Bible we call the New Testament. Our next stop will be there. It is in the New Testament that the final lessons about submission are taught.

But before moving on to explore this powerful relationship with the Creator, we should do two things. First, we should take a closer look at the strategy of the rebels as it affects us in real, twenty-first century time. Second, we need to settle on what submission is, and just as importantly, what it isn't.

Knee Deep in Trouble

Imagine you are visiting South America. There you are strolling along the shore of the Amazon River. Can you think of any reason you might not want to wander knee-deep in the shallows? That's right, Piranha, ferocious little fish that have been known to devour an unfortunate cow in minutes—eating it alive. In the muddy water, you don't know whether a bunch of hungry little fish are lurking nearby. Best to stay high and dry rather than allow part of your anatomy to be vulnerable to a school of piranha.

Now, imagine that you *have* to walk knee-deep in the shallows, and it's just the way it is—no other option; life is lived with part of you just naturally under the water where piranha can get at you. Give you the creeps? Does me. If that's the way it was I'd be on the lookout for anything "fishy" in the water. And that's a little what it's like to be human. Time-creatures live with part of their nature submerged, as it were, in the heavenly places. Instead of legs, ankles and feet, it's their soul—mind, emotions, and that "intuitive sense" which is what's left of our spirit, the original link with the Creator. The spirit was originally hard-wired to the Creator, essentially making his ways and the choices of the time-creatures virtually inseparable, but in its damaged state, it is tuned to the lower frequencies of the heavenly places. Soul and damaged spirit, these are the non-physical components of human nature. By original design they were bi-dimensional, that is created to be useful in both time/space and in the infinite/eternal. In wartime, they are the "submerged" parts of human nature that are vulnerable to the rebel weapons.

The advantage to the elohim piranha is the same as to the fish: they have the ability to lurk unseen, and then attack one or more of the vulnerable appendages, in this case human spiritual attributes. Their weapons in this warfare are stealth, deception, manipulation, and fear. This rebel army may be imprisoned, restrained and disembodied, but that doesn't mean it isn't dangerous, particularly when it operates without most time-creatures even knowing it exists.

Does that mean that whenever we feel afraid, angry, hurt, aggressive or any of a dozen unhealthy emotions, that we are being attacked by demons? No. Sometimes there is direct involvement between the elohim and those intangible parts of our nature, but usually our responses are our own. I have a feeling, though, that most unhealthy responses are the residue of past attacks that have become part of our mental and emotional conditioning, so much a part of our decision making that we aren't aware of how we began to make our choices in the way we do. In short, unhealthy choices and responses may be habits that we adopted during earlier attacks from the heavenly places.

The way this looks in real-time varies: irrational fears; "hot buttons" in our lives that somehow "get pushed." We'll respond poorly to a situation and later say, "I don't know why that made me so angry." Or, "I don't usually panic like that..." Sometimes our minds, consciously or subconsciously, wander back to hurtful or frightening experiences to the extent that those past situations become the means by which we make present decisions.

The bare mechanics of all this is a mystery. Stranded here in time/space we are left to draw what parallels we can from our experience—demons shooting arrows into our mind and the like—but full understanding of how this all looks from the far side of the dimensional boundary will have to wait. The important thing to remember is that there are parts of our humanness that are vulnerable to varying degrees of intrusion from the spiritual side of existence. In the worst scenarios humans have been known to be virtually controlled by an aggressive rebel fighter—or many of them.[1] More commonly, we live in shadows of past encounters that have shaped our reactions and our choices.

Submission is about reshaping those patterns by a repaired and empowered spirit interface with the Creator, replacing those old responses with new ones. How is that done? First, by reconnecting the human spirit, and then by tuning in to the Creator's frequency—hearing Him—and then practicing obedient responses. Once we are empowered to know the Creator's will, then practice and repetition brings us into sync with His original design. That, in its simplest terms is submission. And that is why this concept is one that the rebels have been most careful to attack.

What it is...or not

In the last chapter I pointed out that for millennia we have been abused by a Nimrodian understanding of submission, an

---

[1] Jesus encountered such a case in Matthew 8.

understanding that is only a half-step removed from the ancient deceptions that got the first humans tossed out of the garden. Let's not keep making the same mistake.

Jody remembers arriving in Alaska to speak at a women's conference. A friend that she had known for years picked her up at the airport. Immediately, they launched into the usual how-ya-doin-whatcha-been-up-to chatter until they were almost to the friend's house. That's when the conversation got around to the conference.

"What are you teaching this weekend?" the friend asked as they made the turn into her driveway.

Jody remembers taking a deep breath before answering, "Submission."

She may as well have dropped a glass of ice water into her friend's lap. The friend said she doubted she would be attending the conference.

That response wasn't surprising. Subjection, submission, authority, and leadership are terms that have been used, abused, misused, and confused so often that a rumor that the pastor is preaching on submission next week can create more empty pews than Super Bowl Sunday. The whole concept of submission has been twisted, and here's how.

Most of us are used to approaching this subject with one question in view: Who's the boss? Along the way we look for some practical tips on how to be dominant—graciously. We hope to learn how to be passive—graciously. But we often get the uncomfortable feeling that somebody had better be toeing the mark or somebody's head will be graciously rolling.

But, submission before it became a casualty of relationship in the garden, was supposed to be directed toward the Creator. In time/space it wasn't to be practiced as a hierarchy—one above others—but an "heirarchy." The subtle transposition of two letters changes everything. It creates a new word that describes a community of heirs—fellow heirs. It describes a kinship of followers who are learning to walk together as subjects of one King, becoming skilled at the ancient and lost art of submission. Fellow heirs do not rule and dominate each other, but learn from the King himself what it means to follow as subjects. The community that results is *heir-archy* a subject that I'll talk about in more detail later.

When we were growing up, the TV Western was the staple of prime time. The Lone Ranger and Matt Dillon, Dodge City and the OK Corral, cattle rustlers and train bandits were icons of what was called the Wild West. "Bringin' law 'n order to the town" was the theme of countless books, TV shows and movies.

The equivalent in Israel's history (here's one of those places where the children of Abraham have something to teach us) was the time of the Judges. Attacking bands of Canaanites were the bad guys, rustlers and "Injuns" in those days, and the Hebrews were the "settlers." As in the old West, ancient Israel needed a little "law 'n order." Twice in the Old Testament book of Judges the time is described this way: *In those days there was no king in Israel; everyone did what was right in his own eyes.*[2] The descendants of Israel repeatedly plunged into sin and anarchy, while God, by his astonishing mercy, repeatedly delivered them from ruthless marauders that were the consequence of their disobedience. Against the background of such moral chaos it is tempting to lay the blame on a lack of strong central leadership. We would like to interpret the aforementioned passages as if they read, "In those days there was no king in Israel, *[therefore]* everyone did what was right in his own eyes."—as though a monarchy was the solution to the problem.

But earthly kings were not God's preferred choice. The story of Israel's first king, Saul, makes it clear that the installation of a king was, as it were, against God's better judgment.

As I suggested earlier, biblical history confirms that when God grants a request reluctantly there are grave consequences. In the book of Exodus, the descendants of Israel complained

---

[2] Judges 17:6; 21:25.

about the lack of variety in their diet as they wandered in the wilderness. God had been giving them manna, and that had been fine for a while, but there came a time when the novelty had worn off and they craved meat. God granted their request, underscoring his reluctance with the promise that if it was meat they wanted, then meat they would have—they would have meat coming out of their nose! But in Psalm 106, it is noted that, though God had granted their request, the end result was "leanness of soul" for the people of Israel. Their flesh may have been satisfied, but their spiritual life—weak in faith— was malnourished.

It is a similar situation that occurs at the end of the period of the judges. The book of 1 Samuel describes the response of Samuel, the high priest, as the people demand a king.

> But the thing was displeasing in the sight of Samuel when they said, "Give us a king to judge us." And Samuel prayed to the LORD. And the LORD said to Samuel, "Listen to the voice of the people in regard to all that they say to you, for they have not rejected you, but they have rejected Me from being king over them." [3]

Appointing an earthly leader, a king, was seen by God as a sign that the people were more eager to be in subjection to a man than to their God. Nonetheless, he instructs Samuel to grant their desire, but with a solemn warning of the consequences of their error (see 1 Samuel 8:11-19).

This suggests an intriguing question. If God was opposed to a monarchy for his people, what did he prefer instead? The fact is He proposed no alternative, leaving us to infer that God was quite content for the people to live within the system of the judges that was already in place. It would be a mistake to conclude that the monarchy of Israel is a good model for leadership, authority and submission. Evidently, the opposite is true.

---

[3] 1 Sam 8:6-7.

The problem with a system in which, "everyone did what was right in his own eyes" was not the lack of a king—God was the King of Israel—the problem was the *lack of subjects*, people who were in submission to their Creator King. By demanding a king, they chose to submit to somebody like themselves rather than relearn the skills of subjection that had been forgotten that dreadful day in the garden.

We continue to make the same error if, when we think about submission, we think of a game plan for husbands or a guidebook for wives instead of our relationship with the Creator. Submission is not merely a recipe for marriage or an operations manual for churches and organizations. To limit the message of submission in that way is far too narrow. God's invitation to submit is extended to all who are willing to respond to The Seed in anticipation of what lies beyond, and that doesn't include our flawed interpretation of submission.

Two Imposters

Two imposters often pop up as we try to grasp what the Bible says about submission, subjection, leadership and authority: domination and passivity. We presume that God's main concern when it comes to submission is who is the boss; who's at the top of the heap; who leads, and who follows. When subjection becomes disconnected from the One to whom subjection is ultimately due, we become less concerned about what it means to follow God than with the world inside our own skulls, and with our interpersonal relationships.

My children gave me an exaggerated understanding of this when they hurled themselves into the teen years. I watched astonished, as the bathroom mirror became the focal point of the universe. Before their hormonal crisis came upon them, they were oblivious to their appearance. Suddenly they were spending a significant part of their day critically evaluating themselves in front of the mirror. There, they attempted to predict how their hair, clothes, smile, nose, or the dreaded zit, might impact their social prospects. I was constantly amazed at

83

what embarrassed them. They were abashed because they were too short. Humiliated by something called "spaghetti arms." Mortified that we drove a used Ford. Scandalized at the thought of putting their lunch in a paper bag with the name of the grocery store on it.

Adolescent insecurity is not new, of course. The first attack occurred in the Garden of Eden. It was just after the "forbidden fruit incident" that Adam and Eve became "embarrassed" enough to put something on. Hmmm. Maybe God inadvertently created the first humans as teenagers? A better explanation is that our relationship with God directly affects how we interact with the community around us. Joined with their Creator, Adam and Eve were confident in themselves and their place in the garden. Alienated from Him (the consequence of their unwitting alliance with rebel elohim) they were furtive and self-conscious and alienated, not only from God but from each other.

That alienation has played out generation after generation. The first followers of Jesus (The Seed) are a case in point. Jesus had a fully operational "spirit interface" with the Father. Based on the rock-solid security of that relationship, He was the model of humility and servanthood. In contrast, those first twelve students were often found arguing about which of them was greatest. While their Master served and patiently taught, the disciples were found vying for the places of prominence, imagining themselves as leaders of the nation, even calling down fire on dissenters.

These students, called disciples, were spiritual adolescents. They were uncertain of their place and their value in the Plan that was unfolding before them. They exhibited the disoriented behavior of their fallen race. So do we. If we are not confident in our relationships most of us become introspective and self centered. We tend to see ourselves through the eyes of those around us. We become an insecure actor in a one-person drama, fearing the critics, while earnestly hoping for a standing ovation. Lacking the place of intimacy with God that we were designed to have, we shrivel in fear or strive for recognition.

A popular sermon illustration tells the story of the captain of a merchant ship who had an ongoing feud with the chief engineer. Each was of the opinion that his job was the most vital to the operation of the vessel. Both had made it quite clear that they felt the other's job was the proverbial piece of cake. Finally, one of the crewmen suggested that the two trade jobs and put each other to the test. Then came the day of the grand experiment. The two men worked mightily, each at the other's post. Eventually, the captain staggered out of the engine room, covered in bunker oil from head to toe, and one hand bandaged with a greasy rag.

"You win," he declared in exasperation, "I can't make her go."

The haggard looking chief engineer appeared at the railing on the bridge and hollered back, "It don't matter anyway. I ran her aground!"

If the captain and chief engineer had kept their places, the ship would have stayed on course. Trying to expand their own worth and assume responsibility for which they were not suited got them and their seagoing kingdom into hot—make that shallow—water.

Adam and Eve unwittingly entered into a similar arrangement. Ignoring their proper place, they imagined that they could assume responsibilities for which they were not prepared. They were enticed by one of the elohim who was in the same state of delusion.

The leader of the rebellion in the eternal dimension (the heavenly places) is sometimes called Lucifer. Biblical scholars frequently apply the description in Isaiah 14:4 to him. In that passage, Satan's self-aggrandizing goes as far as, "I will ascend above the heights of the clouds; I will make myself like the Most High." Such babbling may sound like hopeless delusion, but it seems whenever pride and arrogance are in full bloom, the curious will be drawn to the fragrance. A variation of Satan's delusion was enticing enough to lure Adam and Eve.

The Snake wanted to be at the top of the heap—the king of the hill. He wanted God's creation to be subject to him, therefore, he refused to be subject to God. He then went on to infect the human family with his rebellious disease, deceiving them into a predicament little better than his own, with the exception that *his* condition was hopeless. Had Eden's citizens understood the situation, it's difficult to imagine they would have willingly gone ahead in their disobedience, but the Scripture says they were deceived. As they were lured into Lucifer's inimical world, they thought they were getting independence. What they got was domination by Satan.

The calamity of temptation isn't what they were tempted *by*; it was who they were tempted *from*. It was Lucifer's successful deception that shorted out the wiring of the human heart, blowing two critical circuits. The first, was man's open link to eternity. That, in turn, overloaded the circuit that empowers our ability to reflect God's image in our relationship with each other.

There is an important thing to understand. *Humans were created to be submitted to the Creator.* In their unspoiled condition they would reflect the cooperative, consummate image of God in their relationships. But they became rebels. They chose not to be in subjection to God who is the only one worthy of it. Having discarded the only legitimate object of their submission, humans loosed that unmet need on each other and their relationships began to deteriorate into rivalries and conquests.

It is as though our need to be in submission became a "loose end" begging to be tied up somewhere—anywhere.

Tying Up Loose Ends

In the Northwest, rock climbing is a popular sport. There are several locations near our home where climbers can be found challenging sheer rock walls. Hanging between heaven and disaster by what looks like a thread, is exhilarating to some. To me it looks like lunacy. In spite of my opinion (or perhaps because of it) my son dabbled in the sport for a time. We watched with clenched fists and knotted stomachs as he scaled a rock wall with two other climbers.

The lead climber, who was experienced in climbing technique and had done the climb before, made her way up the face of the cliff, choosing the safest route for the group. Another climber followed a dozen feet below, fastened to her by a rope. Caleb was roped last. As they inched their way up, the lead climber would fix a protective anchor in the rock, to make sure that she and the ones below were roped securely to it in case of a slip. As she tied off the rope she would yell encouragement and directions down to the other climbers. Occasionally, if Caleb missed the instructions, the second climber would repeat them for him. The safety of the climb was in the hands of the experienced lead climber.

What would have happened if the one in the middle had thought, "I'm tired of being a follower. I don't care if she does know the route. I want to be in the lead. Let the kid down below follow me for a change!" What if he reached up a few feet and cut the rope that connected him to the lead climber and the security of the anchor she had set? Now, he's free from any connection with the lead climber, and so is the climber below. So, what does he do with the loose end of the rope, the one that used to be tied to the lead climber? Common sense would argue that he should tie it somehow to something secure—the cliff face—to guard against an accidental fall; that done, he would begin to lead the hapless climbers that were unfortunate enough to be roped to him, securing himself to the cliff as he went.

The "common sense" of creation is that humans also should be securely tied to something. There is a place for that in the Creator. We, like the middle climber, are supposed to be tied to our Creator. The "rope" that was supposed to connect us is *willing submission*. The rest of creation was to be tied to the

Creator through us. That's the relationship that God described when he said, "fill the earth, and subdue it...and rule over everything that moves on the earth (Genesis 1:28) ."

When the "high end" connection with God was cut, humankind instinctively sought to attach it somewhere. Paul's letter to the Romans describes where.

> Professing to be wise, they became fools, and exchanged the glory of the incorruptible God for an image in the form of corruptible man and of birds and four-footed animals and crawling creatures.... For they exchanged the truth of God for a lie, and worshipped and served the creature rather than the Creator, who is blessed forever.[4]

Just as that middle climber would have secured himself to the face of the cliff, humans in their deceived, disconnected state quite naturally turned their instinctive need to be in submission toward the creation, including other time-creatures. That shift is called *idolatry* and it was the natural outcome of rebellion.

Just as our need to be in subjection to God is "hard wired" into our nature, so is our capacity to rule. The rope of subjection, secured in God, was to run downward through Adam, Eve and their descendants, toward the creation. God's "common sense" order was an unbroken line of submission through which human hearts, in partnership, would govern creation. When that line was broken, worship turned to idolatry and, after the pattern of the rebel commander, humans (remember Nimrod) began to unleash their capacity to rule on one another. Submission was to have been born into the human family bearing the likeness of the unified nature of God himself. Instead, domination, and her deformed twin sister, passivity, came forth to despoil divine order. From these spring brutal kings and oppressed peoples; playground bullies and terrified children; ambitious executives and injured egos;

---

[4] Romans 1:22-23.

tyrant husbands and timid wives; from these come destructive hierarchies and abused congregations.

As the power to relate to God was cut off in the garden, so was the power to walk in submission with other people.

Domination and passivity have nothing to do with submission. In fact, they are exactly NOT what subjection is about. They are opposed to the central feature of the human character that is distinctly *in His image:* the ability to choose— more than that, the *requirement* to choose. Called "free will" or "volition," the capacity of human beings to *decide,* to make a conscious and intentional choice, is essential if men and women are to function as God-breathed beings. *Submission is the appropriate exercise of God's gift of choice.*

Adam started out in submission. He ambled about his pristine world free to choose. Adam's advantage prior to the "the incident" was that he had an open line with the Creator by which he could discern whether his choices were good ones or bad. In Genesis, the most notable instruction concerning the relative goodness of a decision was in verse sixteen of chapter two. "From any tree of the garden you may eat freely," said God, "but from the tree of the knowledge of good and evil you shall not eat, for in the day that you eat from it you shall surely die."

Good advice. For the time being, Adam chose to heed it.

Immediately following those instructions, in verse 19, Adam had another choice to make. It was at that time that God "formed every beast of the field and every bird of the sky, and brought them to the man to see what he would call them; and whatever the man called a living creature, that was its name."

Responding and Initiating

In his time of innocence, Adam demonstrated the two roles in godly submission, the role of the responder, and the role of initiator. As a responder he was free to follow the instructions of the Creator, which he did. (Later, he used that same freedom to disobey.) As an initiator, Adam acted within the will of God when he named the animals.

Domination does not express submission. Why? Because it reaches beyond the personal world of the initiator and preempts the choices of those around him. Far from initiating the will of God, one who dominates destroys the ability of others to freely choose. That takes away their capacity to reflect God's image.

Passivity does not qualify as an expression of submission, either, because it renounces the element of choice. If God had made Adam merely passive, the man would have had no real choice regarding the tree—or anything else, for that matter. The first time-creature would have been an organic robot unable to respond to God and reflect his image.

Several years ago, we were called upon to counsel a couple that was struggling with their family life. Both husband and wife had become followers of Jesus in the early seventies and had received considerable teaching about authority and what was called, "chain of command." Much of that teaching concerned "covering" and implied, sometimes commanded, the husband's unquestioned authority in the home. The husband in the pair we were counseling was, by temperament, a controlling personality, and the wife's disposition tended to be passive. Based on the teaching they had been receiving, they were a "match made in heaven."

Believing that his dominating nature was exactly what God had in mind when scripture talked of a husband being the head of his home, this husband proceeded to "rule his household." While he tinkered with his computer and practiced guitar, his wife dutifully cooked and cleaned. When his job demanded that he work swing shift, he got his household up at four in the morning so they could enjoy "family time." Meanwhile, in the name of submission, his wife quietly attempted to satisfy the demands of her husband's "leadership." As time passed, she became burdened and depressed. When she attempted to express her concerns and discomfort, the result was a one-sided filibuster that inevitably wore her down to the point of capitulation. The husband's interpretation of these "discussions" was that they had come to an agreement on the issue. She would accept the situation with resignation, then comfort herself in the knowledge that "at least I'm submitting to my husband." The fruit of this relationship was pain, the deterioration of the woman's personality, broken sexual behavior, angry and discouraged children, and, ultimately, divorce.

The couple pursued this distorted behavior for years thinking that to do otherwise would in some way compromise biblical order. In reality, their conduct—both the husband and the wife's—did not reflect the image of God. The husband, in a quite ungodly fashion, disfigured God's image when he dominated his family, denying them the freedom to be in partnership with him by eliminating their choice. Not only did he not reflect the merciful character of the Father, but also he made it impossible for his marriage to reflect God's fully cooperative, multi-faceted nature.

She, on the other hand, passively, grudgingly, accepted the situation as though to have no opinion was somehow a reflection of the bride of Christ. Eventually, her frustration became so unbearable that she sought an escape from the marriage. Other women with dominating husbands have suffered physical abuse when they finally refused to continue in what amounted to marital servitude. We aren't suggesting what course of action is best in these situations; only that passivity is no more a reflection of subjection than dominance.[5] Neither of them are appropriate interpretations of submission. Domination is not appropriate for an initiator of God's will because it does not cooperate with Him in preserving the freedom and dignity of others. Passivity is not a

---

[5] It should be noted that dominant behavior can also be exhibited by women, often through manipulation and emotional coercion. When it comes to distortions of biblical subjection, neither men nor women hold exclusive bragging rights!

valid quality for a responder, since it abdicates God's gift of choice.

The husband and wife in this example could have acted in harmony with God's original intentions. According to their own confession, they were "saved"—Jesus had repaired the broken wiring of their hearts. Tragically, they never stopped relying on the heightened non-spirit senses that the time-race has relied on since the beginning. A new way—really the original way—was available to them, but they never unlearned the distortions of domination and passivity; hierarchy and coercion. They never actually understood submission.

Greek is the original language of the New Testament. The Greek words for submission do not demand a hierarchy. One such word, *hupatasso,* literally means to be put in order, or to arrange in an orderly fashion. Depending on how it's used, it may describe a dependent position or a relationship to superiors, either compulsory or voluntary, but in the New Testament the word often does not carry the thought of being controlled and following orders.

Peter, one of the early students of Jesus wrote "...all of you be *subject* one to another"[6] and another disciple, James, said, "*Submit* yourselves, therefore, to God..."[7] In both cases, the issue is not "who is the boss" but how *we respond* to others, whether they are in authority or not. When it comes to submission, the key question is not who should lead, but *how we should follow*. This is a vital lesson to learn because Jesus has reconnected our spirit to the Creator who intends for us to follow as the first of our kind once did.

In order to do that, we're going to need some practice...and someone to demonstrate what to do. Fortunately, both are available.

---

[6] 1 Peter 3:5.
[7] James 4:7.

Chapter 6

Perfume on the Latch

In a way, the story of the Creator, the rebellion in heaven, and the alienation of the race of the time-creatures is a love story, the love story from which all other love stories are drawn. Two lovers (the Creator and his creation) are parted in a cruel deception and swept away from one another by the winds of war. The husband, in his passion for his lost love, devises a daring plan to rescue his beloved from the clutches of ruthless captivity. Does this sound like a familiar story? Of course it does. Variations of this plot have been played out in novels, plays and films. It is one of those timeless narratives drawn from the very core of human experience. It's part of the meta-narrative of creation.

Not surprisingly, the children of Abraham, Isaac and Israel illustrate that aspect of history in the writings that we know as The Song of Solomon, a book of romantic poetry attributed to Solomon, a Jewish king who lived close to a thousand years before the coming of The Seed.

This moving portrayal of love is a prophetic anticipation of the coming of The Seed, the coming of Jesus. It is an allegory in which the king represents Christ and the woman, his beloved, represents the race of time-creatures that he seeks to win. It tells of the yearning of the Creator for his "bride." It also speaks of the inborn yearning of humanity for a renewed relationship with Creator-God. Here is a sample. The first speaker is the bride.

> I was asleep, but my heart was awake. A voice! My beloved was knocking:
>
> "Open to me, my sister, my darling, My dove, my perfect one! For my head is drenched with dew, My locks with the damp of the night."
>
> "I have taken off my dress, how can I put it on again? I have washed my feet, how can I dirty them again?
>
> My beloved extended his hand through the opening, and my feelings were aroused for him. I arose to open to my beloved; and my hands dripped with myrrh, and my fingers with liquid myrrh, On the handles of the bolt.
>
> I opened to my beloved, but my beloved had turned away and had gone! My heart went out to him as he spoke. I searched for him, but I did not find him; I called him, but he did not answer me.[1]

In these verses the perfume on the latch becomes a symbol of the bride's awakening passion for relationship. Her desire propels her on a frantic search for her lover who, thankfully, desires more than anything else to be found. It is a search that begins with the voice of the Bridegroom—an invitation to relationship.

In the garden of Genesis 3, God's invitation came as soon as the relationship had been carelessly thrown away. I wonder how Adam and Eve felt when they began to understand the awful consequence of their foolish choice? The shame! The horror! The hopelessness! To face the reality of their lost relationship with God must have been overwhelming. Yet, from our vantage point in history we realize that the condition of the human race was not hopeless because God had already begun His plan to reestablish relationship with His bride (humanity) through "The Seed." God said to the serpent, "And

---

[1] Song of Solomon 5:2-6 (NASB).

I will put enmity between you and the woman, and between your seed and her seed; he shall bruise you on the head, and you shall bruise him on the heel."[2] The first hint of God's passion to restore the broken relationship with humanity was right there in the garden. The Seed of which He spoke would be His own Son who would suffer the bruises of an earthly death, only to rise up and crush the head of the rebellion, the snake, Lucifer, Satan. The promised Seed is the Bridegroom-Creator gently knocking on the door of the bedchamber, the human heart.

Out of the ruin of broken relationship rises a glorious truth: God wants us back! He will spare no expense to accomplish redemption. Beginning with the prophecy in the garden, God has acted as the earnest lover and "extended his hand through the opening" seeking His bride. He has continued to do so ever since. The question has always been, will she—the human race— respond?

The story begins similarly to this section of Song of Songs:

> ~The Bridegroom yearns for his bride. (God wants us back.)

> ~He extends His hand. (The promised Seed is an invitation to a restored relationship.)

> ~The bride hesitates to respond. (God's people repeatedly fail to grasp his invitation because of what the Bible calls a hardened or "darkened heart.")

But at the coming of "The Seed" who is Jesus, the love story of God and his wayward creation takes a remarkable turn: The Bridegroom comes and demonstrates an unbroken relationship with the Father. He then *gives His bride "new eyes"* with which to see and learn.

Jesus' followers learn to see with new eyes and turn from their old ways.

---

[2] Genesis 3:15 (NASB).

In the meantime, over the centuries, the Creator uses the nation of Israel to constantly remind his bride of the sorrows of estrangement and the promised joy of reconciliation. Remember those markers and symbols? They are like pictures.

A Picture of Relationship

On the side of a church building in our area, there is a gigantic painting. A casual glance could leave one with the impression that a free-spirited art student has expressed himself in bold swatches of black and white that resemble a map of some obscure chain of islands. For months I passed that church, each time regarding the strange mural as a mere curiosity. Then, one day, as I rounded the corner and the building came into view, the black and white spots unexpectedly, almost magically, formed a coherent whole. There on the broad white wall of the church was the face of Jesus, his eyes extending a haunting invitation to passing motorists. It had been there all along. I simply hadn't "seen" it.

Similarly, God's invitation to restored relationship emerges from experience of the descendants of Abraham, Isaac, and Israel. From the first time we meet Abraham in Genesis, to the coming—the second coming—of Christ, The Seed, in the Book of Revelation, divine parables unfold. God, like a Master Artist, paints the mural of history. It is "*His* story," the passion of what has been called, "the divine romance." Illustrated by peoples and nations, kings and commoners, families, friends and lovers, the relationship that was lost in the garden is seen on the canvas of the centuries. The cycle of desire and estrangement that started when Eve was tempted and Adam joined her in sin, has been rehearsed and magnified again and again as humankind, the "bride of creation," repeatedly rejects the headship of God, her "eternal Bridegroom." Though she instinctively yearns for Him, the covert warfare of the rebel army constantly resists.

Beginning with the battle in the heavenly places, more stories emerge. They exhort and encourage us; rebuke and chasten us. In the Song of Solomon, God woos and ravishes; His bride yearns and responds. Elsewhere, human defiance spills across the pages of Scripture in bloody calamity as those who are not humbled before God become those who fall. Repeatedly, God invites relationship and man responds, but before the relationship can become defined, the fallen elohim manipulate mind and emotion, spoiling the invitation. Cycles of deception, temptation, and rebellion begin again.

The events in the Bible teach the principles of submission and authority in patient, though sometimes brutal exposition. As characters—often briefly—humble themselves in subjection to their God, peace and rest appear. As God's people defy the Creator's plan, and go their own way (a replay of the treason in the garden) war, destruction, and heartache explode across the land.

As the history of Israel unfolds, we hear the cry for reconciliation rising from the heart of God. His voice resonates from the eternal depths—each event, with a slightly different inflection:

"What is this you have done?" In the garden it is the voice of anger.

"I am sorry that I have made them..." At the flood, there is the voice of despair.

At the tower of Babel, there is frustration. *"They are one people, and they all have the same language. And this is what they began to do..."*

But then, the emphasis changes. In the story of Abraham, often called the father of faith, is heard a murmur of hope. "Go forth ...to the land which I will show you," the Lord declares to Abram. "I will bless you...you shall be a blessing...all the families of the earth shall be blessed." The words turn Abram's gaze toward a homeland—a type of Eden. There he will become the father of nations, become a patriarch, and be bound by covenant. But, like the garden, the homeland will be abandoned. Abraham's children will flee in a time of famine and not return for over 400 years. Then, Abraham's "Eden" will be called the "land of promise." It will elude his children just as the garden of our first parents eluded them—even as an unbroken relationship with the Creator has eluded us. Indeed, after the people of Israel, a nation of slaves, enters the land of Abraham's covenant, they will be unable to live there in peace. Such is the lot of unsubmitted people who abandon the inheritance of their God.

Lessons of the Unsubmitted

So, what can be learned about subjection from unsubmitted people?

God calls Abraham to be in subjection to Himself and offers a covenant relationship, symbolized by circumcision. Again and again God gives Abraham the opportunity to submit to Him. Sometimes those tests end in failure. Others, as Abraham's near sacrifice of Isaac, declare his triumph in faith. *From Abraham, we learn that we are to be subject to God in our utter dependence upon Him as our provider.*

A few generations later, a man named Joseph and his brothers are jealously divided over a series of dreams. In the dream of the sheaves, the brother's sheaves bow down to Joseph's—a visible act of submission. His brothers resent the thought of coming under rule so, in reprisal, they kidnap and sell Joseph into slavery.[3]

While enslaved, Joseph rises to a position of favor only to be slandered and thrown into prison where he learns submission through the things he suffers there. Eventually, Joseph's family comes and bows in submission to a ruler of Egypt. As it turns out that ruler is Joseph who providentially risen to a high office in Pharaoh's court. Joseph is given all power and authority in the kingdom, all the while in submission to the authority of Pharaoh. *The story of Joseph reminds us that we are required to be subject to God as King, and that our spirit must govern the flesh.*

---

[3] Genesis 37.

Moses lives under the benevolent authority of Pharaoh, the king of Egypt, while the Hebrews languish in slavery.[4] Moses submits to God's call and direction and God displays signs and wonders through him, defeating Pharaoh's idolatrous power which refuses to acknowledge the Creator's authority. As the descendants of Abraham, Isaac and Israel flee Egypt they cease to be subject to evil authority and are called to be subject to God. Once out of Egypt, and on their journey in the desert, the Israelites rebel against God and challenge Moses. They resist submission by their stubbornness and their appetites, paying the price with death and wandering. *The Israelites explain by example that if we will not learn submission in the role of a slave, we will learn it in the crucible of freedom. If our life is not ruled by spiritual truth it will be driven by our fleshly habits.*

After Moses' death, Joshua obeys the Lord and brings the land of Canaan under submission to the Hebrews, but Israel doesn't completely turn from worshiping idols, so she becomes bound to the worship of pagan gods. *Misplaced submission ultimately leads to sadness and desolation.*

Throughout the Scriptures the stories unfold. The book of Judges reviews the painful 70-year cycles of a nation vacillating between wanton rebellion and desperate remorse. The account of First and Second Kings traces the tragedy of one rebel ruler after the other. Throughout, the voices of the prophets repeatedly call the nation to repent and submit to God, just as our spiritual nature, if it's properly submitted to God, is supposed to call our soul and body to obedience. Jesus, himself, joins the prophetic chorus as he laments the broken chain of submission saying,

> "O Jerusalem, Jerusalem, who kills the prophets and stones those who are sent to her! How often I wanted to gather your

---

[4] Story begins in Exodus 2.

children together, the way a hen gathers her chicks under her wings, and you were unwilling." [5]

Downward Spirals

Such wearying trials of waywardness! In the first chapter of Paul's letter to Rome, the apostle summarizes the consequences of such persistent error. First, he describes his task: "to bring about the obedience of faith among all the Gentiles, for His name's sake." To be obedient is to willingly submit one's self to the will of another. In the chapters that follow, Paul identifies Christ—The Seed of Genesis 3—as being the one in whom faith could be placed. Christ's ability to save and empower, says Paul, makes Him able to break the cycle of depravity that has strangled the world since the beginning.

Then, in verses 18-25 the apostle describes the downward spiral—the dreadful consequence of people living outside the life-giving sphere of a submitted relationship with their Creator. It all begins with the *rejection of truth*. In verse 18 Satan's lie is revealed to be always the obstruction of the truth of God: "For the wrath of God is revealed from heaven against all ungodliness and unrighteousness of men, who suppress the truth in unrighteousness…"

That was certainly the case in the garden when Satan questioned the motive of God regarding the tree, and cast doubt on God's truthfulness concerning the outcome of disobedience. It is that same disruptive spirit that came to be part of the programming of fallen human kind. Consider Cain. [6] He murders his brother, yet when God confronts him and asks about his brother's whereabouts, Cain answers, in effect: "How should I know? He's not my responsibility!" Less than a generation removed from the conception of Satan's treachery, and already the reflex of human nature is to suppress the truth rather than be subject to it!

---

[5] Matthew 23:37 (NASB).
[6] Genesis 4.

In Romans 1:19 and 20 Paul says,

> …that which is known about God is evident within them; for God made it evident to them. For since the creation of the world His invisible attributes, His eternal power and divine nature, have been clearly seen, being understood through what has been made, so that they are without excuse.

The facts about God were staring Adam and Eve in the face—with the wonder of the garden all around, that seems like a no-brainer—yet they still fell for deception. Time-creatures have been repeating that pattern ever since. That same mindless insistence on sin causes otherwise sensible people to do utterly senseless things. "I knew I shouldn't be alone with him," said a young Christian woman, remorseful over a moral failure. "He wasn't a believer. He was sometimes crude. But he was just fun to be with…" She knew what God's best looked like, but in spite of her commitment to Christ, she suppressed that internal leading. The facts were evident, yet she defaulted to the old post-Eden program rather than to God's operating system.

In verses 21-22 the apostle addresses the next downward step, *futility*.

> For even though they knew God, they did not honor Him as God, or give thanks; but they became futile in their speculations, and their foolish heart was darkened. Professing to be wise, they became fools…

My husband, Dan, can be quite handy. He has to be because our household is typically a low-budget operation. Over the years we have saved a modest fortune thanks to his "do-it-yourself discount." The down side of his resourcefulness is that he sometimes gets in over his head. Link that with his all-too-male tendency to refuse to ask questions and you can expect a wiring repair job to plunge the house into darkness before it's done. He doesn't profess to be wise, he just doesn't confess to being uninformed. He doesn't admit to being foolish, he humbly suggests that he's on a "steep learning curve" that, at times, feels like futility. As he's fond of saying, "Good judgment comes from experience. Experience comes from *bad judgment*."

Our first parents tinkered with the wiring of their spirit. The foolish hearts of their willful descendants have been regularly darkened by futile speculation ever since. It has something to do with trying to plug our spirit into an incompatible power source.

When we visited Israel a few years ago, we borrowed some electrical adapters from some friends. The adapters, we were told, would be necessary because the power supply there is different than in the States. After our morning shower we plugged the hairdryer into the adapter, and the adapter into the wall. Then we turned on the dryer. If I hadn't been holding it tightly it might have gone airborne. Fortunately, we were able to turn it off before it exploded or activated the Israeli air defense system. Clearly, our American hairdryer was incompatible with Israel's power grid.

The human spirit is incompatible with any power source other than the Spirit of God. That hasn't kept our race from attempting to "plug in" to other sources, though. Paul identifies those unsuitable spiritual sources in verses 23-25.

> ...and exchanged the glory of the incorruptible God for an image in the form of corruptible man and of birds and four-footed animals and crawling creatures. Therefore God gave them over in the lusts of their hearts to impurity, that their bodies might be dishonored among them. For they exchanged the truth of God for a lie, and worshiped and served the creature rather than the Creator, who is blessed forever. Amen.

Rejection of truth leads to futility and futility is one degree of separation from idolatry. The worship of idols is the key indicator of rebellion throughout the Bible. Idolatry is the evidence that the elohim have twisted human minds and emotions so thoroughly that they have rejected the Creator. Idolatry is when the rope that is supposed to be secured in the

Creator has been cut and tied to the time/space dimension. It is the ultimate rejection of God's influence. The perpetrator of the garden lie that took human beings from under the Creator's authority and harnessed them to idols, still persists in his treachery, even here at the turn of the twenty-first century. Idolatry may not look exactly as it did then, but it is just as pervasive. Materialism, celebrity worship, leisure, and pleasure are part of a pantheon of gods that belie their poisonous spiritual content. 2 Tim 3:2-5 describes these latter-day idols, rival lovers who lure the bride away from her beloved:

> For men will be lovers of self, lovers of money, boastful, arrogant, revilers, disobedient to parents, ungrateful, unholy, unloving, irreconcilable, malicious gossips, without self-control, brutal, haters of good, treacherous, reckless, conceited, lovers of pleasure rather than lovers of God; holding to a form of godliness, although they have denied its power...

No matter what shape an idol may have, a false source of authority is a poor trade for the truth of God.

Misplaced submission has warped our perception of the concept into something contrary to God's. But, just as there is much to be learned about submission from unsubmitted people, there is even more to be learned from the One who walked fully in submission—who chose to "humble Himself, taking the form of a bondslave."[7] With the "first Adam" come lessons by trial and error. From "the last Adam," that is, Jesus, The Seed, come lessons by *trial and truth.*

Paul identifies Jesus, the gift of God's righteousness, as the only hope for learning the better way. By *trial and truth* Jesus has brought us like raw recruits into the basic training that is called faith. It is there we are to learn its key precept, submission. And it is *from there* that we are to take up the weapons by which we will defeat, once and for all, the enemy

---

[7] Philippians 2:5-8.

of creation and enter into the relationship for which we were created.

Historians will debate long and loud over the United States' involvement in the Middle East. There will be arguments over weapons of mass destruction, troop strength, readiness, sectarian rivalries in the region and covert alliances. That is the way it is with every conflict. Rearview analysis is standard. The debates usually boil down to whether the key players on the global stage made the right decisions. What should Iraqi commanders have done when faced with the buildup of American firepower? What should the Americans have done when faced with the unexpected resilience of the insurgency? There will be endless discussion of the strategic successes and blunders.

One has to wonder if there will be similar talk when the war between the rebel elohim and the time-creatures is won. I doubt it. But as I write this, the eternal war is still going on. There is a rebel army amassed just over the border between time and eternity; to defeat it will take more than just the awareness that it is there. We understand its tactics. There has been a resilient insurgency going on since Genesis 6. But since then, two things have been changed. First, The Seed of prophecy has come and nullified the legal entitlement of the enemy force to the time-race; consequently, the human spirit can be "switched" on. Secondly, the time-creatures have been resupplied with new and better weaponry, heavy artillery called submission.

But a high-tech weapons system is useless if the troops don't know how to use it. Before victory there is preparation and training.

We watched an interesting thing happen when our son joined the army and went through basic training. At first, he (and probably every other recruit) hated the drill instructors. At the end of "basic" that hatred had turned to admiration for those same gravel-voiced drill sergeants that had driven them to exhaustion during boot camp. By the time the grueling weeks of preparation were over a genuine affection had developed. That was particularly true toward the instructors that had seen combat. There was something about receiving instruction from experienced warriors that made the agony of basic training endurable and made the recruits want to emulate their trainers.

Even now the Creator is preparing an army of time-creatures, a human army, to bring an end to the elohim insurgency. He has put the responsibility for training in the hands of The Seed, Jesus. He is a combat veteran, a living lesson who has fought in the trenches facing and defeating death. He demonstrated by example the secret of a fully responsive spirit. He is skilled in the use of submission, the weaponry of this war. He will teach us those skills just as he experienced them himself, by taking on three roles:

~ The role of the child submitted to the parent.

~ The role of the slave submitted to the master.

~ The role of the husband toward a bride.

These don't sound very formidable, but this isn't a war like we usually think of war. With these weapons Jesus fought bravely and victoriously. Now, it is our turn to enter the fray, but before we do, we have to learn firsthand, the skills of submission. Our performance in battle will depend solely on how carefully we have observed the Master's skill and craft. And *that* will depend upon how strongly we desire the restored relationship that the Creator has made available. If we want it badly enough, we need to enlist, report for duty and prepare for "boot camp."

PART 2

Boot Camp

Chapter 7

An Apparent Need for Parents

His parents didn't know what to think. "Son!" his mother said to him. "Why have you done this to us? Your father and I have been frantic, searching for you everywhere."

"But why did you need to search?" he asked. "You should have known that I would be in my Father's house." But they didn't understand what he meant.

Then he returned to Nazareth with them and was [in subjection] to them; and his mother stored all these things in her heart. So Jesus grew both in height and in wisdom, and he was loved by God and by all who knew him.[1]

Most parents know the sudden panic when a child is lost. Our most vivid experience was at a lake not far from our home. We had been chatting with friends as we sat on a blanket near the water so we could keep an eye on our young children. Suddenly, when we looked up to take inventory of the kids, we couldn't find Corrie, our middle child. We bolted for the water's edge, searching frantically for her, first among the playing children then, terrified, in the water. While Dan desperately walked in a zig-zag pattern in the murky water, I ran, calling her name, to the nearby bathhouse to see if she might possibly be there.

---

[1] Luke 2:48-52 (NLT).

She was. We had become so engrossed in our conversation that none of us had noticed her as she walked by. Our relief can't be described.

The experience helps me imagine the emotions of Mary and Joseph as they searched for Jesus—I relate to them on a personal level.

Submission as "Kid Stuff"

This story, however, does more than merely awaken parental empathy. It is more than a dramatic vignette in the childhood of The Seed. Jesus' detour to the temple reflects the singular passion of His life. Just as importantly, it places His zeal in the context of submission. He patiently explained his actions to His parents, then went home and lived obediently— the eternal bridegroom, submitted to his human guardians who were from the race that is to become his eternal bride.

Jesus learned (taught) submission in the school of childhood.

Parents are the initial relationship where we learn submission. From them we learn how to yield to a will other than our own. A healthy understanding of that kind of yielding only comes when trust has developed. In the best circumstances, that relationship emerges as the nurturing of the parent makes the child feel secure and confident.

My childhood (Jody) was not like that. My parents divorced when I was about four, and as I have grown I have realized how significant that event has been in my development. At that young age I learned that the most important people in my life were not always there. I had to wait for the weekend or the next holiday if I wanted to interact with one of them face to face. As the only child from my parent's marriage I grew to feel more and more like the outsider as they went on to build new lives and new families.

This kind of broken image of the parent/child is a product of "the Eden incident." Sadly, it's not uncommon. Very few of us see an accurate picture of the nature of the heavenly

Father's love for his children in our earthly families. What we call "the fall" has left us with gaps and distortions that make it difficult to understand what dependency should really look like. If we weren't living in a world disconnected from the Creator, we would learn subjection in our natural experience. Our tendency toward operating in the strength of our soul—our willfullness—would be curbed, and the strength of our spiritual character would mature.

Few of us were fortunate to be raised in an environment that taught us healthy submission. That doesn't mean that our experiences are useless for learning, however. Indeed, contrast can be a great teacher.

In counseling, Jody will often require homework that she calls "The Father Assignment," in which she asks the one she is counseling to list the qualities of a perfect father. When they return for the next visit, she asks them to share their list with her and identify which of the qualities they experienced as they were growing up. Not surprisingly, very few of the qualities on the list are a part of their real experience. And that is the goal of the assignment, to invite them to turn to their heavenly Father and ask Him to be the parent in a way that their earthly parents could not. It is a lesson in contrasts.

In the same way, the contrast between our experience and the way Jesus was able to interact with his Father can help us learn how to walk in subjection. By observing Jesus in the parent/child relationship we can learn that wisdom, humble obedience and the ability to intuitively respond to the Father's will (what could be called "response-ability") are three qualities of Godly subjection.

Subjection as Wisdom

The story of Jesus in the temple concludes with these words: *Then he returned to Nazareth with them and was in subjection to them.... So Jesus grew both in height and in wisdom.* The result of being in submission to his earthly parents was that Jesus gained wisdom. That early training taught him how to harmonize his behavior with the will of his heavenly Father. John, the apostle, who was moved so deeply by the knowledge that Jesus loved him, was also profoundly impacted by the love that Jesus had for his Father in heaven. John carefully noted the nature of that father-son relationship and was deliberate to use Jesus' own words to describe it. In John 5, the apostle quotes his Lord:

> Truly, truly, I say to you, the Son can do nothing of Himself, unless it is something He sees the Father doing; for whatever the Father does, these things the Son also does in like manner. For the Father loves the Son, and shows Him all things that He Himself is doing...[2]

We remember our children begging their father to let them push the lawnmower. Occasionally, Dad would let them try, and the sight of a toddler trying to push a machine three times his size was as amusing as it was futile. Ironically, by the time they became physically able to mow the lawn, they were no longer interested in imitating their father's behavior!

In contrast, Jesus, the submitted son, was a careful observer of the Father, and a faithful imitator. That is a picture of wisdom. Paul calls Jesus "God's mystery...in whom are hidden all the treasures of wisdom and knowledge."[3] Just as wisdom is personified in the 8th chapter of Proverbs, Jesus' example of subjection to the Father becomes the living embodiment of wisdom and wise behavior in the New Testament.

But an important reality is often overlooked. The life of Christ is more than just a metaphor for wisdom; it is in fact, wise life—*connected life*. It is the life of subjection that was intended *for all humankind*. That's why Paul in his letter to the church in Corinth, uses a common rabbinical expression to identify Jesus: "the last Adam."

---

[2] v. 19-20.
[3] Colossians 2:3.

The psalmist said, "the fear [reverence; honor] of the Lord is the beginning of wisdom."[4] In a real sense, the fear of the Lord is actually the *regaining of wisdom,* since wisdom was precisely what was lost in the garden. Romans 1 could have been the life story of Adam (the first one, that is) and Eve:

> For since the creation of the world His invisible attributes, His eternal power and divine nature, have been clearly seen, being understood through what has been made, so that they are without excuse. For even though they knew God, they did not honor Him as God, or give thanks; but they became futile in their speculations, and their foolish heart was darkened. Professing to be wise, they became fools...[5]

The resurrection of the human spirit is the reversal of that tragic consequence. Jesus accomplished that on the cross, by his own death and resurrection. From that point "the foolishness of the cross," as Paul said, became the wisdom of God—the road back to the connected life. Jesus lived that life fully so that we, in our new life in Christ, would know what it looked like, and by the Spirit, be empowered to regain it by subjecting ourselves to the Father as he did

Six times John records Jesus saying that He could not do anything on His "own initiative," but only those things that He saw, heard, or learned from His Father. Jesus was a dutiful responder to God, as was the pre-fall Adam. Jesus was careful to execute the Father's instruction.

But Jesus was also a model *initiator;* He acted on the Father's will because He knew His Father intimately. Interestingly, when John records that dimension of submission, he recalls these words of the Lord:

> For this reason the Father loves Me, because I lay down My life that I may take it again. No one has taken it away from Me, but I lay it down on My own initiative.[6]

---

[4] Psalm 111:10.
[5] Romans 1:20-22.
[6] John 10:17-18

When Jesus acts on *his own initiative,* he lays down his life. From that description we learn that walking in submission means presenting a humble, sacrificial character.

Submission as Humble Obedience

In Philippians chapter two, Paul remarks about the humble character of the Lord Jesus. His observation is that Jesus' humility was the quality that made it possible for him to be "obedient to the point of death, even death on a cross." The writer to the Hebrews makes a similar observation, only applying it to the Lord's role as a son: "Although He was a Son, He learned obedience from the things which He suffered."[7]

The word for "obedient" means to be attentive, literally, "to hear under." The picture is of an eager listener, hanging on every word of a superior, ready to take action at the first opportunity. Such is the picture of submission that Jesus models.

Our son briefly took karate lessons. The instructor was called a Sensei, which is a title that means something like "man who can rip off your ear with his toes if you don't show some respect." In a no-nonsense introductory speech, theSensei explained that early martial arts training is mostly careful observation of movements, followed by relentless, sometimes painful, repetition. This was a disappointment to Caleb who imagined that fighting thugs and splintering fence posts with his bare hands would be fairly easy after a couple of lessons. Because he wasn't ready to practice the Sensei's instructions until they became a reflex, Caleb's aspirations to be the next Chuck Norris were short lived.

"No pain, no gain," has long been the aphorism of coaches, athletic directors and military officers. The most successful athletes and soldiers drive themselves through pain in order to learn necessary skills. For that reason, a good drill sergeant

---

[7] Hebrews 5:8.

sets goals that are beyond the boundary of the soldier's personal comfort. After a week of "PT" and marching with full gear, the soldiers may gripe and complain, but the best ones know that obedience through the pain of training may make the difference between life and death when it counts.

In the end, willing subjection to the one in authority leads to instinctive obedience and the efficient execution of the skills learned in training. By willingly subjecting Himself to His Father, Jesus modeled a life of perfected obedience.

Subjection as Response Ability

As Jesus showed by His relationship with the Father, a restored relationship with God begins with godly wisdom. Secondly, Jesus demonstrated that following the will of God requires humble obedience even beyond our personal comfort. Now, after the pain of laying down our own lives comes the ability to respond to the will of the Father. According to Paul that amounts to nothing less than living like Christ.

> I have been crucified with Christ; and it is no longer I who live, but Christ lives in me; and the {life}, which I now live in the flesh I live by faith in the Son of God, who loved me, and delivered Himself up for me. [8]

We probably won't have much success consistently responding to the will of God unless we are willing, by His Spirit, to let Christ live in us. From that indwelling life comes "response-ability." It has to do with intimate knowledge of the will of the Father.

Perhaps that is what Jesus had in mind when he taught us to pray.

In the Lord's Prayer, one of the first things that Jesus instructs His hearers to say is an expression of worship—"hallowed be Thy name." Making room for Christ to live in us so that we can have the ability to respond to God's will begins with worship.

---

[8] Galatians 2:20.

One of the great things about choosing to follow Jesus is the recognition of the love and awesomeness of God. That's a fitting place to begin learning to do His will which is the impetus behind the words, "Thy kingdom come, Thy will be done…" Learning worship paves the way to knowing what the Father wants done and then doing it. Furthermore, the exercise of God's will is the only authentic extension of genuine worship. In the prayer, when Jesus instructs us to "call His name Holy," He is simply calling us to worship. From that starting point, He tells us to ask the Father for the coming of His kingdom, which is where, as we would expect, His will is done.

For a long time I imagined that God took those requests for His kingdom to come and wrote them on His "to do list" as though they were a worthy, but premature suggestion. Yet Jesus often spoke of the kingdom as though it were a presently expanding reality. He even said that the kingdom was presently "among" His listeners. It's worth noting that all the requests in the Lord's Prayer are for immediate concerns— daily bread, present forgiveness, ongoing deliverance. Is the request for God's kingdom to come any different?

That depends on our understanding of the nature of God's kingdom.

After the terror attacks on the World Trade Center, we became very familiar with life in Afghanistan. After the Soviet withdrawal from a disastrous war there, Islamic revolutionaries rose to power. Suddenly, under the Taliban, a new government took shape that changed the direction of the nation. A militant, religious zeal began to be enforced. Western influences were condemned, women were required to abide by strict Islamic law, and the political landscape came under the watchful eye of the Islamic religious establishment. Almost overnight, the population became subject to the will of the Taliban. Within the borders of Afghanistan, Taliban edicts were binding. Comparable conditions existed in Iraq under Saddam Hussein.

Eventually, that kind of rule was dislodged in both nations leaving them to struggle to come under a new government.

If the kingdom of God were a geographical entity, God's edicts would be binding within its boundaries. But God's kingdom is not geographical; it is spiritual. The boundaries of His kingdom are fluid. They are continually redrawn to include wherever His will is done.

The mechanism for extending the kingdom of God on earth is submission. Just as Jesus acted as an obedient *responder* to God's direction, and as a faithful *initiator,* we are to choose to exercise our freedom in ways that are consistent—in harmony—with the Father's character and intention. It is Father God's goal to execute His will on earth as it is in heaven by raising up a race that will act as He would want them to, and as He would, Himself—people who will serve Him and worship Him in obedience. That submitted response is what it means to *exalt* the Father.

The dictionary definition of 'exalt' is, "to glorify, praise, or honor; increase the effect or intensity of something." It means to put something in the best possible light.

Recently, we went out to dinner with a pastor friend of ours, and his wife. When we stopped to pick them up, we were greeted at the door by their teen-age daughter who welcomed us graciously and invited us in. After dinner at a restaurant, the four of us returned to their house where we enjoyed a time of pleasant conversation. Once again, their daughter greeted us at the door, and as we were getting settled, asked if she could get us something to drink. Presently, she brought us some tea and ice water, joined the conversation for a time, and then slipped out to attend to other matters. We were impressed by the young woman's poise and hospitality. Her maturity and friendliness made us feel completely at home. As I commented to the parents about her, they nodded proudly and affirmed that their daughter was a great joy to them.

Two things were true about our experience that evening. First, the parents were pleased with their child. They took great pleasure in her. Secondly, I couldn't help but regard the parents with respect. Naturally, I assumed that they must be admirable people to have produced such an admirable child. By her behavior, this young woman had *exalted* her parents.

The same two things are true when the children of God behave in submission to His will. Because of their obedience, He is pleased and proud of them. In addition, when God's children display honorable character, those who observe their behavior are convinced of the worthiness of the Father. Doing His will as we walk in submission to Him, exalts God.

To exalt the Lord is to shine a bright and positive light on Him, revealing Him truly and fully. It would be letting ourselves off too easy to limit the vocabulary of exaltation to mere words. Exalting God requires a whole-life expression that begins with an understanding of ourselves as children. A restored connection with God will play itself out much like the relationship between parent and child. To learn parent-and-child-submission is to begin loosening the tether that binds us to the world. The lesson begins when we rediscover what it means to see God as a Father. Then by worship and voluntary subjection—Christ living in us— we bind ourselves to Father-God and He begins to pry us from the world's stubborn grip so we are free to do what He wants done.

The Challenge of "Child-Likeness"

Relating to God in this way is difficult for many. We travel often to assist with Pastors' Prayer Summits.[9] Frequently,

---

[9] Prayer Summits, through *International Renewal Ministries* are a four-day worship and prayer experience for pastors and Christian leaders. These events are worldwide in scope and are characterized by a "no agenda" approach that frees participants to pursue the Lord together in prayer, fellowship, and worship. The goal of the summits is to facilitate a sustained move of God in the regions that host them, by facilitating an encounter with the holiness of God that leads to genuine humility, spiritual unity, genuine community, and ultimately, city impact.

participants are encouraged to respond in prayer to the person of God, the Father. Dan reports that this is often very difficult for the men. Pastors confess to being able to relate to God as Savior, or as King, but to respond to Him as a loving father is a challenging, often emotional experience. Yet if we don't learn how to be subject to God as Father, how will we know His will clearly enough to do it? It appears that there is much we need to learn from Jesus about this, starting with what it means to be childlike.

Jesus was a student of childhood, an astute observer of kids. He often used them in His illustrations. He upbraided the religious establishment for their childishness when He compared them to children playing in the marketplace. Conversely, He exhorted His disciples by encouraging them to be more childlike in their response to faith.

> And He called a child to Himself and set him before them, and said, "Truly I say to you, unless you are converted and become like children, you shall not enter the kingdom of heaven. Whoever then humbles himself as this child, he is the greatest in the kingdom of heaven. And whoever receives one such child in My name receives Me..." [10]

What a precious picture! Jesus, surrounded by adults, focuses on the children! In this case, Jesus needed an example of a quality that was essential if the lives of His followers were to exalt the Father. He needed an illustration of humility, and the kind of humility He was looking for was the innocent humbleness of a child. As usual, He didn't have to go far to find one. The message was simple: People cannot truly exalt God and walk in pride, any more than they can call Jesus, "Lord," and not do as He says...and as He *does*.

In His childhood detour to the temple, and in His adult responses to His Father, we observe Jesus in the role of a Son. We are to carefully note His attitudes and behavior, then imitate what we've seen. That would be simpler if the roles of

---

[10] Matthew 18:2-5.

119

parent and child in our lives were anything like the relationship that Jesus had with His earthly and heavenly Father. But whether by comparison or contrast, the Lord's experiences tell us as much about the meaning of living in submission.

Jesus took great satisfaction in discerning the Father's will and then doing it on earth as though it were in heaven. As he modeled this subjection He honored God and painted a complete picture of His authority as Creator and King, but the image that emerges most clearly in the Gospel of John is that of God as Father. Jesus' pattern of behavior makes it clear that He found more joy by investing His free will in submission to His Father than in any selfish purpose.

As we reflect on the way Jesus modeled the role of a son as He interacted with His Father, we are to observe, learn, imitate, and practice Jesus' responses until we are transformed in the way we think—what the Bible calls the "renewing of the mind" (Romans 12). Only then will we be able to discern God's will clearly enough to do it and overcome the covert efforts of the elohim who want nothing more than to prevent us from living in the love of our Father where the true power of being human is found.

Chapter 8

My Master, My Mentor

Be dressed for service and well prepared, as though you were waiting for your master to return from the wedding feast. Then you will be ready to open the door and let him in the moment he arrives and knocks. There will be special favor for those who are ready and waiting for his return. I tell you, he himself will seat them, put on an apron, and serve them as they sit and eat! He may come in the middle of the night or just before dawn, but whenever he comes, there will be special favor for his servants who are ready! (Luke 12:35-38)

Learning subjection as servants is a vital paving stone on the path to a reconnected life. It challenges us in ways that are different from the lessons of sonship, but no less vital. One of the tragedies of modern evangelical life is that believers enter into their relationship with God as servants, and only later—sometimes never—as children. This is tragic because the focus of the master/slave relationship tends to be on what we do rather than who we are. When we experience those periods of laziness and mediocrity, as we inevitably do, we are filled with feelings of uncertainty about whether we've lived up to God's standard of performance and are still acceptable to Him. To play the slave without understanding the joyous assurance of the child is discouraging, and an incomplete picture of our relationship with God.

Christ as a son, demonstrated how to act *like* the Father, but Christ, the servant, teaches how to act *on behalf* of the Father. The child's role draws life from simply being—we *are* children. The servant, on the other hand, learns to defer his own purposes to those of another. The will of the master is the duty of the slave. The focus of the slave becomes how he spends his time, and on what. His purpose in life is defined by what he does; and his value is drawn from the one for whom the work is performed.

In the first phase of training, Jesus demonstrated how to wield the power of sonship. Now, he takes up the weapon of servanthood.

The scene opens on a hot day by a village well. Jesus' disciples return from a brief trip to buy food and discover that their teacher has been conversing with a woman. This alone is outside acceptable social limits but to make matters worse the woman was a *Samaritan*—a religious half-breed, despised by observant Jews. They are shocked. Still, this is their Master. All the disciples can think to do (after an awkward silence, I imagine) is suggest that the Lord eat some of what they brought. Jesus responds, "I have food you don't know about." It is as though He wants to force the disciples to comprehend His unusual behavior. His men register a collective, "huh?" to which Jesus returns, "My food is to do the will of Him who sent Me and to accomplish His work."[1]

Jesus' words bring practical import to the injunction of Deuteronomy which he used in a battle of wits against the elohim commander: *man shall not live on bread alone, but on every word that proceeds out of the mouth of God*. To Jesus this was not pious talk, but sober practice. In essence, Jesus had said, "I would rather follow the Father's instructions than eat." This was the lesson He wanted His disciples to learn as the human "harvest" poured out of the nearby town to see Him who had spoken to one of their women at the village well. The disciples needed to learn the lesson of the bondslave: when the Master assigns a task, there is great joy and fruitfulness for the servant who is prepared to accomplish it.

Jesus, our instructor and commander, has much to teach about the submission of a servant. First, a servant submitted to God is not a slave by compulsion, but a bondslave—one willingly indentured in a contract of love. But a slave cannot

---

[1] John 4.

be truly submitted unless he is able to respond—simple willingness isn't enough. A servant in subjection must be two things:

> Prepared for the work.

> Available to the master, ready to act when he says the work needs to be done.

Submission Means Being Prepared

I (Dan) liked the movie, *Karate Kid*. OK, it wasn't academy award winning cinema, but what can I say? I liked it. There is something winsome about the story of Daniel, the lonely, fatherless teenager coming of age, who befriends the apartment maintenance man, an older Okinawan gentleman. Fortunately for the young protagonist, who has a knack for irritating the neighborhood karate bullies, his new friend, Mr. Miyagi, happens to be the best kept secret of the martial arts world. The story moves predictably through the young hero's tribulations with the school thugs, to the inevitable showdown at the karate tournament. But before the climactic battle, "Daniel-san" must learn to fight!

Mr. Miyagi puts Daniel to work. Paint miles of fence: "Brush up! Brush down!" Wash and polish a fleet of cars: "Wax on! Wax off!" Sand acres of cedar decking: "Sand right! Sand left!" Finally, tired, frustrated, irritable and belligerent, Daniel explosively announces that he's through being the slave. That's when Mr. Miyagi reveals what all that seemingly irrelevant work was really leading up to. Unbeknownst to poor Daniel-san, each repetitive motion has been part of a key move in karate, stuff so basic that he needs to be able to do it in his sleep.

You don't need me to finish the tale. The plot is, after all, predictable. But an important concept shines through this charming, albeit simplistic, Hollywood story. In order to get good at something, preparation is the key. People spend hours rehearsing medical scenarios so they can save lives as paramedics. My auto mechanic draws on years of mechanical know-how each time he lifts the hood of "Taurus Gump" our trusty, if slightly rusty, family car. I have had my hair cut by the same stylist for the last 15 years. Each person is prepared for their work.

I have often been intrigued by what have been called the "silent years of Christ." Jesus lived in relative obscurity for nearly thirty years before He began a ministry that was to span barely three. I try to imagine the slow turning of those days. The interminable predictability. Waking, working, sleeping; Passover, Pentecost, Feast of Tabernacles…season to season. Yet, it cannot be said that those years were wasted. In the same way that a doctor or an engineer spends time in preparation for their chosen fields, The Seed labored in preparation for his appointed tasks. He waited as one in training. From His parents and through His life experience He gleaned obedience and knowledge, learning subjection as He anticipated the word of the Master: "Now is the time! Go! Live in full subjection to Me as all humans were meant to live! Show a mirthless people what fully-animated spiritual life looks like. Then, by your death and resurrection, re-energize the circuitry of the human spirit that went cold and lifeless so long ago in Eden." At the end of His brief earthly ministry, Jesus said to His Father, "I have brought you glory on earth by completing the work you gave Me to do" (John 17:4 NIV). As a son, He glorified the Father by His wisdom, obedience, and ability to respond; as a servant, He fulfilled the work for which he had prepared at the time He was called upon to do it.

Christ's pattern clearly made an impact on His followers. Like the headwaters of a river, His "servant example" began to flow through the New Testament and carve a course through God's people. Paul appeals to the Corinthians as a servant, "on behalf of Christ." He refers to Epaphras as one who had taken up Jesus' mantle of servanthood on behalf of the brethren in Colossae. The imagery of the bondslave repeatedly appears as the redeemed of the Lord learn to imitate the behavior of their master.

But useful servanthood comes after a time of preparation—for Jesus it was nearly thirty years, for Paul, it was fourteen.

As a young believer I (Jody) remember growing restless as I dreamed of doing a great thing for God. I was anticipating the coming of the Lord; I had the sense that I was wasting time, missing opportunities, failing to walk in fruitfulness. I worried that the final trumpet would sound and I would be found at the starting gate, not having begun the race. I felt guilt for my uselessness. Of course some of those feelings are normal, but the years have added some perspective.

Joy Dawson, whom I respect as a teacher, and a mature woman of God, has observed that, "more is accomplished in five days of genuine, Spirit-led revival, than in five years of intense human effort." Given her vantage point in maturity, Joy has noted that much effort is squandered by young believers who have not prepared themselves as servants while waiting for the call of the Master. The issue is timing. When berries are ripe, they are easily harvested. Un-ripened berries are difficult to pick. Aged wood splits with less effort than green, newly-felled logs. Daily life is filled with examples of things that require preparation before they are ready. For Christians, that means waiting and practice, taking care to give both their proper weight.

Dallas Willard in his book, *The Spirit of the Disciplines* makes the point that we often mistake spiritual disciplines as offerings to God to secure His favor when, in fact, they are preparatory. They make us ready and able to respond to God. Paul instructed Timothy, his younger protégé, to "be diligent to present yourself approved to God as a workman who does not need to be ashamed, handling accurately the word of truth." In his letter to the church at Ephesus, he described the preparatory nature of the work of the spiritually mature in the churches (Ephesians 4). Their work was for, "the equipping of the saints for the work of service, to the building up of the body of Christ; *until we all attain* to the unity of the faith, and of the knowledge of the Son of God, to a mature man, to the measure of the stature which belongs to the fullness of Christ." (Emphasis mine). We often miss that huge word, "until" which suggests that there is a time for preparation and a time when the believer ought to be ready to assume responsibility.

A Means to What End?

Sadly, this preparatory feature of submission can be misunderstood and abused. In churches and households, subjection can be treated as an end in itself; a means of establishing and maintaining order and assuring that someone is "in leadership." That notion is so strongly ingrained in the thinking of some that to suggest something different is to be branded "unsubmissive" or "in rebellion." What is needed is a thorough reconsideration of submission. When it is understood as remedial training for redeemed people—arming them for spiritual warfare and re-fitting them for kingdom citizenship— it loses its hierarchical sting.

Jesus, knowing that His disciples were prone to delusions of power and prestige, was careful to describe submission clearly. Moreover, He established its great importance by choosing to illustrate it at the Last Supper. Of all the concepts He might have chosen to teach during those waning minutes, He chose to emphasize leadership by servanthood.

And He said to them, "The kings of the Gentiles lord it over them; and those who have authority over them are called 'Benefactors.' But not so with you, but let him who is the greatest among you become as the youngest, and the leader as the servant. For who is greater, the one who reclines at the table, or the one who serves? Is it not the one who reclines at the table? But I am among you as the one who serves (Luke 22:25-27).

Contemporary interpretations of leadership and authority notwithstanding, submission isn't about "who's the boss?" On the contrary. From Jesus point of view, it is about serving in the Master's name.

To the disciples the memory of Jesus kneeling before them, washing their feet, must have had a profound effect. "If I then, the Lord and the Teacher, washed your feet," He told them, "you also ought to wash one another's feet. For I gave you an example that you also should do as I did to you." His words apparently penetrated deep into their souls because the tradition of selfless service, what Christians call ministry, emerged immediately among the believers when the church was born.

The early church understood that ministering to the hungry, thirsty, ill-clothed, and to prisoners was work ordained by the Lord for them to do. Jesus' student, Matthew, remembers Jesus making it clear that these were the ones that His disciples needed to be prepared to serve,[2] and in so doing, serve Him. In a sense, Jesus was training His followers to act as His surrogate among the poor; to serve them as He would, acting on His behalf.

In the New Testament, the word for "ministry" is the word from which get the term "deacon" and refers to labor that has purpose. Among Christians, it often reflected compassionate work toward the needy within the community. More broadly, every business or calling, so far as it resulted in some benefit for others, was termed "ministry." The idea of effectual work for others was woven into the fabric of the church from the very beginning and has persisted. Until recently, few traditions were more widely recognized as distinctly Christian. Take a mental inventory of the hospitals and colleges near you. In most American cities, if the names of such places do not bear a clearly Christian influence (e.g., St. Vincent Hospital or Good Samaritan) their histories often do—evidence even today, that the Master's call to service has been heard consistently among Christ-followers.

Jesus emphasized that leadership in the church was not measured by status, title or power, but by being willing and able to serve. The servant-heart that stopped beating in Eden

---

[2] Matthew 25.

was resuscitated at Calvary, and is strengthened when we, as redeemed people, practice submission as servants.

Paul comes at the issue from a different direction, from the standpoint of those consigned to follow. He instructs Titus a local church leader to, "remind [Christians] to be subject to rulers, to authorities, to be obedient, *to be ready for every good deed,* to malign no one, to be uncontentious, gentle, showing every consideration for all men" (Italics mine).[3] Note that Paul's emphasis in the context of obedience is readiness. He exhorts Titus to use the servile circumstances in which they lived as a teaching tool to prepare them for living in God's kingdom as bondslaves of the King. He then contrasts the old, disconnected life of an expatriate of Eden with the redeemed life of one with a reconnected spirit:

> For we also once were foolish ourselves, disobedient, deceived, enslaved to various lusts and pleasures, spending our life in malice and envy, hateful, hating one another. But when the kindness of God our Savior and His love for mankind appeared, He saved us, not on the basis of deeds which we have done in righteousness, but according to His mercy, by the washing of regeneration and renewing by the Holy Spirit, whom He poured out upon us richly through Jesus Christ our Savior....[4]

In the life of the servant, then, submission works itself out in two ways. First, in *becoming prepared to be useful* for the tasks that lie ahead and, once prepared, being found *ready and available to respond* when the master speaks.

Submitted and Available

It was Thanksgiving Day and what I (Jody) really needed was one of those turkey basters. You know, one of those long plastic tube things with the rubber bulb on one end that slurps liquid out of a roasting pan. The pan was streaming turkey

---

[3] Titus 3:1.
[4] Titus 3:3.

juice all over the oven, and the before dinner comments had gone from, "Mmmm! Something sure smells good!" to "Is that the smoke alarm?!" Hurriedly, I pulled open the drawer to grab the baster and...where was that thing? Aarghhh! Why can't I ever find a thing when I need it?

It's an all too familiar story.

Dan often complains that a household job always takes twice as long because the tools that he needs (and knows that he has) are not where they are supposed to be. A friend of ours, in a project run amok, came dashing down the steps after having punctured a water line. As water gushed all over his bathroom, and began to drip through the ceiling of the room below he searched in vain for the vital tool which, of course, was not there. It is the curse of a household shared with school-aged kids.

There are times I wonder if God feels that way about me. From his heavenly perspective He watches as circumstances in someone's life come together, ripe for divine intervention. He thinks of my unique blend of gifts that will be just perfect to complete the work He has begun. The moment has arrived. He wants to use me and....arrghh! Where is she *now*?

Theologically, there are lots of holes in the above scenario. God is never caught by surprise. Still a servant is required to be ready. Paul instructed Timothy to, "preach the word; be ready in season and out of season." Peter exhorted the church to be ready "to make a defense for the hope that is in you." The language in these passages describes readiness as, "to set upon; stand upon; be present." It is a picture of one whose attention is turned in a specific direction, like a sprinter who has focused on the sound of the starter's pistol.

A servant must learn to be available. The English word, 'available,' means, "suitable or ready for use. Profitable, advantageous; be of use or worth." In scripture a reoccurring phrase captures well the thought: "Here I am, Lord." Becoming available is an enormous challenge for us as American Christians. Our cultural baggage is weighted down with assumptions about time, priorities and value. Learning to be in subjection as new creatures in Christ is much costlier than most of us realize. If Jesus is our example, then we will have to be prepared to adjust our thinking so that we can live the kind of life He lived. It might best be called "an interruptible life."

Have you ever stopped to notice how much of the ministry of the Savior was done in response to interruptions? In Luke 8, Jesus steps out of the boat after returning from the incident with the Gadarene demoniac and is interrupted by a synagogue official whose daughter is gravely ill. On the way to heal the little girl, a woman who has been hemorrhaging continually for 12 years interrupts Jesus. He stops and heals her while making important observations about the qualities of faith. Later, in chapter 12, Jesus is preaching about persecution and worry when a man interrupts Him saying, "Teacher, tell my brother to divide the family inheritance with me." Jesus stops what He is doing, and responds to the request with teaching about coveting.

Most of us are not very responsive to that kind of life. We want our schedules in place, and the items on our "to-do" lists checked off one by one. We are much more comfortable when our plans are "chiseled in stone" than we are when life just comes at us. We argue that God, in His sovereignty, is capable of using our plans for His purposes, but often this argument is a thinly veiled appeal for God to operate at our convenience. On the other hand, spontaneity is not inherently more spiritual than organization, nor should "being available" be an excuse for haphazard and lazy living. To balance the two we need a pre-established set of priorities by which to evaluate the way we spend our time.

We had to consider our priorities a few years ago when a painful shake-up in the church leadership left us to consider how we were to meet our financial needs. One option was to return to secular work, yet we were convicted that we had clear direction from God to be available to respond to the needs of the people in our house-church community. After praying about the situation, we decided that anything we did for the purpose of making money would have to leave us free to follow God's predetermined direction. Since nobody was likely to need us for ministry at four in the morning, the solution, to our dismay, was to deliver our local newspaper. The decision was informed by our responsibility in the household of God—we needed to be available.

Servants are usually trained for specific duties. They order their lives around those responsibilities. As a servant, Jesus described his obligations when he was at the synagogue in his hometown:

> The Spirit of the Lord is upon Me, because He anointed me to preach the gospel to the poor. He has sent me to proclaim release to the captives, and recovery of sight to the blind, to set free those who are downtrodden, to proclaim the favorable year of the Lord.[5]

When any of those responsibilities collided with his circumstances, Jesus was servant-bound to adjust his situation in order to attend to the Master's will.

The servant is defined by the task that must be performed; consequently re-learning the subjection of a servant usually means making some significant changes in our view of work and responsibility. As I look at my own life I realize that from time to time I behave as though my servanthood is mostly decorative, like one of those little concrete statuettes of a stable hand that adorns the driveway of some homes. But submission is not alive without application. To learn to be responsive to the voice of the Master I have to be trained. That's what ministry—serving in my world—is about. It is meant to be practiced.

---

[5] Luke 4:18-19 (ESV).

Chapter 9

Lord, Pierce My Ear

When our first parents severed their ties with the heavenly kingdom the catastrophe touched two aspects of human purpose. The first was the relationship that men and women were to have with God. Initially, there was to have been an intimate kinship between Creator and creation, like a parent and child or a husband and wife. But there was a second aspect that was nearly as important, the relationship between humanity and the work that God had laid before them. In Eden God had said, "Be fruitful and multiply, and fill the earth, and subdue it; and rule over the fish of the sea and over the birds of the sky, and over every living thing that moves on the earth." He gave his time-creatures *work to do*—the freedom to act on His behalf. He invited them to initiate action on His behalf, discover the joy and fulfillment of discerning His will and doing it.

Thinking back to the story of the Samaritan woman in John 4, we glimpse the joy of servanthood in Christ when He says, "My food is to do the will of Him who sent me and to accomplish His work." At the time, the disciples were still living the legacy of detachment they had inherited as members of the time-race. Eve, their ancestral mother, had chosen the food in the garden, forbidden though it was, over obedience to her heavenly Master. Isn't it ironic that the disciples were preoccupied with the food they had bought while the Lord was being fruitful and multiplying the Kingdom?

But there is a wonderful sense of anticipation in this story. The woman's open reaction to Jesus' message, the anxious curiosity about the coming of the Messiah, and the overwhelming response of the townspeople as they heard the news from this woman of questionable character—they had a sense that something new and important was being revealed. Actually, it was something quite old. Their response was not anticipation as much as an instinctive yearning for their original purpose. Romans 8 describes that deep longing for fulfillment.

> For the anxious longing of the creation waits eagerly for the revealing of the sons of God. For the creation was subjected to futility, not of its own will, but because of Him who subjected it, in hope that the creation itself also will be set free from its slavery to corruption into the freedom of the glory of the children of God.[1]

The Samaritans were no different than any human beings at that time—or this, for that matter. They were constrained to slavery, not to God as was intended but to creation with its corruption and futility. Their hearts were inclined to be connected to their world and not to their God, yet they desperately longed for that different connection. They saw it in this Jewish Rabbi. What they couldn't know was that Jesus was about to make that connection available to the world. Once that was done, they would have the freedom to trade their compulsory subjugation for voluntary submission. The question was, would they? Once they received "the adoption as sons" would they willingly embrace the work of the Master? Will we?

Our life experience is boot camp in which we learn the skills of submission as servants—a potent weapon. Becoming

---

[1] Vs. 19-21.

prepared and available are two steps to effectiveness. Knowing what needs to be done, and for whom, are next.

A Definition Check

If we are to have a clear picture of the kind of relationship that is supposed to exist between the master and his servant it is important that we don't place the role of a slave in universally compulsory terms. Certainly, there are master/servant relationships that are forced, like the brutal slavery of the Hebrews under Pharaoh in the early chapters of Exodus, but that is a far cry from the relationship that is to exist in the household of God. Indeed, the concept of the "bondslave" appears to be what the apostles have in mind as they exhort Christians to live as servants. A description of that kind of "love-bond" between master and slave appears later in Exodus. It is a much better picture of the servanthood that God designed for his creation. Not compulsion and demand, but willing and devoted service.

> But if the slave plainly says, 'I love my master, my wife and my children; I will not go out as a free man,' then his master shall bring him to God, then he shall bring him to the door or the doorpost. And his master shall pierce his ear with an awl; and he shall serve him permanently.[2]

The scene of a slave presenting himself to his master for the purpose of piercing his ear makes the idea of becoming a bondslave a bit more intense. Admittedly, piercing has become common in modern fashion, but common or not, I approach with reluctance the idea of thrusting sharp objects through my person. If the slaves in Old Testament times had similar misgivings, the act would certainly be a sign of devotion.

Based on that imagery, Jesus appears as the quintessential servant. He set himself daily to fulfill the Master's will and purposes, dying to Himself and His plans in order to do so. He not only served consistently, He performed the sign of the

---

[2] Exodus 21:5-6.

bondslave, the piercing, figuratively in his subjected life, and literally on the cross. Similarly, believers are to return their will to God. This is often called "dying to self" and is captured in Jesus words, "not My will, but Thy will be done." This is the action of a bondslave—the piercing if you will—to signify willingness to be in total submission to the Master by love.

Perhaps this is why God does not insulate us from temptation. Most of us have wished that God would "just make me do right" or would just order our lives by holy writ. Clean and simple, yes, but without the freedom to be "captain of our fate" we would be mere slaves. Still, choice can feel like a constant battle. The New Living Translation gives us a glimpse of the struggle in Galatians 5:17.

> The old sinful nature loves to do evil, which is just opposite from what the Holy Spirit wants. And the Spirit gives us desires that are opposite from what the sinful nature desires. These two forces are constantly fighting each other, and your choices are never free from this conflict.

As *bondslaves* we have something very important to lay before the Master: our freedom. To walk again in a fully responsive relationship with Him as we were designed —this is God's definition of "liberty"—we have to be willing to walk in submission, understanding the will of God and choosing it. Our *"choices are never free from this conflict."* Will we act on His direction today? How about tomorrow? And the next day? Will we choose our own will and our own interests, or will we do what we know is pleasing to Him, daily presenting ourselves at His threshold, ready to be pierced and to bear the ring of the bondslave? If we were compelled by God to do his will, we would be slaves. If we continue to opt for our own will, we become slaves to sin (Romans 6). If we daily lay down our lives for the Master—taking up our cross—we are bondslaves.

But discipleship is costly to the Master, too. Our daily conflict is a reflection of the value God places on His servants. In Second Samuel, the story of David and his plan to build a temple for God, illustrates the point. The land on which David wanted to build was being used by its original owner as a place to thresh wheat. When approached, the owner offered to donate the land. David's response was significant: *"No, but I will surely buy it from you for a price, for I will not offer burnt offerings to the LORD my God which cost me nothing."*[3] The temple through which God would manifest His power and presence was to come at a price. David's act was prophetic of another price that was to be paid by one of his descendants, Jesus.

The temple that David envisioned, grand as it was, would only stand as a reminder of the spiritual life that had been strangled in the garden. In Eden, God's intention had been to accomplish His work through servants who bore in their nature the imprint of His character and presence. The temple, on the other hand, was the Spirit confined, constricted, and quenched—a tragic contrast to the Spirit flowing, unhindered, through fully yielded people.

In the New Testament, the spiritual life of God is liberated from a building. As Jesus, having "humbled himself as a servant," is pierced and yields His life on the cross, the Spirit can no longer be contained in a temple made with hands and hidden behind a heavy veil. As though by a hurricane's blast, the curtain, a symbol of separation, is shredded and the Spirit of God bursts forth like a storm across parched humanity. God energizes again His mortal creations, making them human "temples." Paul reveals the implications of that change in his letter to the church in Corinth:

> "Or do you not know that your body is a temple of the Holy Spirit who is in you, whom you have from God, and that you are not your own? For you have been bought with a price: therefore glorify God in your body." [4]

---

[3] 2 Sam 24:24.
[4] 1 Corinthians 6:19-20 (emphasis added).

Just as the land that David bought became useful after it was purchased, so we, when we were purchased by God at Calvary, became useful—"bought with a price." Servants of God were no longer to minister to God in a building but *from him and by him* in the world. As Paul said, "for it is God who is at work in you, both to will and to work for His good pleasure." [5]

Submission as Action

Just as Adam and Eve were free to either respond to the Master's will, or initiate actions in accordance with it, so we are offered that same choice. It boils down to having the ability to obey. When men and women assume their roles as living temples they are free to *resume their original purpose*. We have another chance to do God's work. As in Eden, we are responsible to discern the will of God and do it. It is up to us to be prepared and available, and then to obey the Master's command.

A.W. Tozer, widely remembered as "a 20th century prophet," speaks of the importance of taking action on the commands of Christ. Says Tozer:

> The sovereign Lord accepts no offering from His creatures that is not accompanied by obedience…the act of committal to Christ in salvation releases the believing man from the penalty of sin, but it does not release him from the obligation to obey the words of Christ. Rather it brings him under the joyous necessity to obey. [6]

Tozer reminds us that relationship with the Creator is vital, but pursuing relationship only, without obedient service—costly discipleship—is to collapse the relationship in on ourselves. The quality of our attachment to our heavenly Master depends both on intimacy and obedience. Jesus said, "If you love Me, you will keep My commandments." The

---

[5] Philippians 2:12-13.
[6] A.W. Tozer, *Of God and Men*, Christian Publications, 1995, p. 52.

submission as children (and bride, for that matter) has as it's natural expression, loving servanthood.

Paul described the dual nature of subjection as he exhorted the church at Philippi:

> Have this attitude in yourselves which was also in Christ Jesus, who, although He existed in the form of God, did not regard equality with God a thing to be grasped, but *emptied Himself, taking the form of a bond-servant*, and being made in the likeness of men. And being found in appearance as a man, He *humbled Himself by becoming obedient* to the point of death, even death on a cross.[7]

In these few verses, Paul observes in Jesus the key elements in the role of the servant: loving service and humble obedience. Learning subjection means to allow these to shape our priorities and inform our decisions in our day-to-day experience. As we apply them, we learn submission and become more and more fit for kingdom living as we do. To the extent that we fail to apply them, our maturity is hindered.

One way that we fail in this regard is as our first parents did: by being tempted away from our first love. Often, sin is less a matter of what we are tempted by, than *Who* we are tempted from. We are just as vulnerable to that mistake now as the first of the time-race were.

Misplaced Submission

There is another way that we fail to exercise loving service and humble obedience: by misplacing our submission. Paul cautions those who were literal slaves in the church at Corinth by saying, "You were bought with a price; do not become slaves of men."[8] His words were intended to remind them that they were enslaved to God first, regardless of their human condition. By having that perspective (God as their only true master) servitude could prepare them for the relationship that

---

[7] Philippians 2:5-8 (italics mine).
[8] 1 Corinthians 7:23.

was unfolding because of Christ's work on the cross. To think otherwise was to misplace submission.

Ironically, Christians today stumble into the same error that Paul warned the Corinthian slaves about—often, in church. Church leaders have long taught submission as a pattern for keeping order in the home and congregation rather than a skill to be relearned as God restores order to creation. To bring about spiritual maturity, submission is to be learned and practiced while navigating the relationships and circumstances that we encounter in life. But if submission is taught as a form, it becomes the basis for structure and hierarchy that readily distracts our focus from the Creator and directs it toward authority figures here in the time/space dimension.

Somehow, this feels appropriate. It feels right because by fallen instinct we are inclined to attach our soul, like the loose end of a rope, to something or someone in this dimension— this fallen world. When a leader cites biblical authority for requiring submission to his leadership we accept the notion unswervingly, or feel guilty if we don't. When a domineering husband cites scriptural justification for demanding obedience from a passive wife, we may struggle with the inequity, but reluctantly, we give way. But this amounts to relational idolatry. It opens the way to a co-dependent relationship between leaders and followers and is the lever that is frequently used to manipulate earnest people in the church.

This isn't to say that there is no room for genuine leadership in the church. Leadership, as one friend of mine puts it, is like breathing, it happens naturally in a body.[9] Watchman Nee in his fascinating study, *The Normal Christian Church Life,* makes some crucial observations about leadership in the church.

> It is important to recognize the difference between official and spiritual authority. In an organization all authority is official, not spiritual. In a good organization the one who

---

[9] My thanks to Hal Miller for this helpful insight. I use it often.

holds office has both official and spiritual authority; in a bad organization the authority wielded is only official.... But in divinely constituted companies of workers there is no organization. Authority is exercised among them, but such authority is spiritual, not official. It is an authority based upon spirituality, an authority which is the outcome of deep knowledge of the Lord, and intimate fellowship with him.... In a spiritual association there is no compulsion; direction and submission alike are on the ground of spirituality.[10]

Watchman Nee understood that submission is never a matter of simple form, but has its roots in relationship with God. Since it acts on behalf of the Creator, real leadership never strays far from submission. Most often we understand leadership to be a visible and powerful role. Surprisingly, though, we don't find it listed among the equipping gifts the Apostle Paul mentions in his letter to the Christ-followers in Ephesus, gifts like pastor and evangelist.[11] Rather, it is found among what are often called "administrative" or "serving" gifts that Paul lists in a letter to the followers in Rome.[12] Leadership properly exercised discerns the needs in the body and facilitates the services that satisfy them. Leadership does not wield authority; it invites it as a response to the ministry (the service) of leading. This squares more neatly with the Lord's instructions about being the least in the kingdom and the servant of all, and contrasts starkly with the hierarchical structures of much of modern evangelicalism. Authority structures obviate healthy growth and participation within communities of believers when disciples are hindered from freely responding to opportunities for submission in their lives. They are denied the maturity that comes from learning subjection. In *The Subtle Power of Spiritual Abuse*, authors David Johnson and Jeff VanVonderen summarize the issue:

---

[10] Watchman Nee, *The Normal Christian Church Life*, Anaheim: Living Stream Ministry, 1980, p. 124-25.

[11] Ephesians 4.

[12] Romans 12.

Each of us has been programmed to look outside of ourselves for the definition of our identity. The behaviors and opinions of others, our own behaviors, the things we collect—all these responses have told us who we are. In Philippians 3, Paul calls this a "mind to put confidence in the flesh".... We have been re-created. This is our new state and identity in Christ. It is this mindset that we must adopt daily to keep from falling into old, entrapping behaviors, or coming under the dictates of spiritual leaders who do not know how to lead us to real life and freedom.[13]

Loving service and humble obedience, can only be learned on the training ground of freedom. Maturity comes only if we can apply these qualities to our life decisions *freely*, not from legalistic motivations or misplaced devotion.

In one of the most poignant episodes in the Bible, the Apostle Paul writes concerning Onesimus, a slave "on the run" in Rome, who had apparently come to faith in Christ through Paul's ministry. Providentially, Onesimus' owner was an acquaintance of Paul in the city of Colossae and a believer, so the apostle pens a letter to Philemon, the slave owner whose name we recognize among the New Testament letters. The letter is apparently carried to Colossae in the hands of Onesimus—redeemed in his spirit, while remaining a slave in time/space. As Paul writes, the qualities of tenderness, mercy and cooperation shine through. He opens the door for Onesimus to serve the earthly master, from whom he once fled, as though he were serving his newfound Lord. His words invite Philemon to die to himself and to submit, in loving obedience to Paul as if to Christ. The picture of submission that emerges is one of willing servanthood, gentle leadership, and life as God's free man.

Therefore, though I have enough confidence in Christ to order you to do that which is proper, yet for love's sake I rather appeal to you . . . for my child, whom I have begotten in my

---

[13] David Johnson & Jeff VanVonderen, *The Subtle Power of Spiritual Abuse*, Minneapolis: Bethany House, 1991, p. 199.

imprisonment, Onesimus, who formerly was useless to you, but now is useful both to you and to me . . . For perhaps he was for this reason parted from you for a while, that you should have him back forever, no longer as a slave, but more than a slave, a beloved brother, especially to me, but how much more to you, both in the flesh and in the Lord. If then you regard me a partner, accept him as you would me. But if he has wronged you in any way, or owes you anything, charge that to my account....[14]

Because of the price that Christ paid on the cross, Onesimus had become a son of God and a fellow heir—part of the "heirarchy" of the church—with Philemon, his earthly master. Their relationship was changed in the time/space dimension and in the eternal dimension for which they were being prepared. Both master and slave learn to trust and obey God the Father Creator, and to serve together as his bondslaves. It is the process we call sanctification: God skillfully blending sonship and servanthood in our spirits in order to restore the free submission to Him that is our heritage.

---

[14] Philemon 8-18.

Chapter 10

To Love and to Cherish

Though I (Jody) am probably not supposed to say so, my daughter, Corrie, looked breathtaking on her wedding day. I had seen her in the bride's room before the ceremony, nevertheless when she appeared at the back of the church, her father by her side, I was struck by how beautiful she looked—positively luminous. The months of anticipation were finally over. The romance that had begun while Corrie was away at college had blossomed and now, surrounded by family and friends, the couple was about to enter into a lifelong covenant. The congregation stood. As Scottish pipes played a haunting melody, Corrie moved down the aisle. When she reached the front of the auditorium, Dan, who also officiated, spoke a blessing, then ascended the platform and began the ceremony.

Visualize the moment. The bride, radiant in her spotless gown, waits at the foot of the stairs. The bridegroom waits for his cue to descend and escort his bride to her father…

Freeze frame.

Let's consider this image for a moment. It is a prophetic glimpse of the future of the followers of The Seed, Christ's bride who is growing in submission as she awaits her bridegroom.

Beginning with the wedding feast at Cana, much of what Jesus taught about the kingdom was couched in wedding imagery, including some of His most beloved words:

> Let not your heart be troubled; believe in God, believe also in Me. In My Father's house are many dwelling places; if it were not so, I would have told you; for I go to prepare a place for you. And if I go and prepare a place for you, I will come again, and receive you to Myself; that where I am, there you may be also.[1]

In Jesus' time, after a couple became engaged it was common for the bridegroom to return to his father's estate to prepare a home for his future bride. The process could take a year or more. Once everything was ready, he would come back to the bride's home, typically at night, to fetch his bride. Surrounded by blazing torches and celebration, the betrothed couple with their friends and family, would make a joyous procession to his father's house, the place of the festivities.

Now, let's return to that day at the church.

The groom descends from the platform to claim his bride. The bride, having made herself ready for this moment, receives her groom. Together, they ascend the stairs and stand before the father. The significance of that picture should not be overlooked. Every Christian couple on their wedding day stands as a living reminder of the destiny of the race that the Creator placed in the dimension of time and space.

Based on that picture, Jesus plays the role of "the eternal Bridegroom" who is preparing a place for his "eternal bride," the church, and will return for her at the appointed time. Paul describes the event in a letter he wrote to the Christ followers in Thessalonica:

> For the Lord Himself will descend from heaven with a shout, with the voice of the archangel, and with the trumpet of God; and the dead in Christ shall rise first. Then we who are alive

---

[1] John 14:1-3.

and remain shall be caught up together with them in the clouds to meet the Lord in the air, and thus we shall always be with the Lord.[2]

The stage is set. For two millennia Paul's description has been alive in the soul of the church. As she waits, anticipating the coming of her Lord, the anxious bride—His people—makes preparations for that day. Through the indwelling Holy Spirit who has resurrected the once dead human spirit, God's people are learning submission so they can rediscover the joy of being cherished children, loved and disciplined; valued servants, bought with a price; and, at last, a bride, betrothed and beloved.

A Submissive Bridegroom

But in the role of bride and groom, according to scripture, there lies "a mystery." The reality of triune fellowship that is at the center of the kingdom of God became a mysterious thing at the point of Adam and Eve's disobedience. The resulting chaos has marred the connection between Creator and creation, and muddled the relationship between men and women.

The blunder of Eden was forsaking submission to the only Being to whom it is rightfully due. It started with Eve when she was deceived toward independence and self-rule, which is the opposite of unity. Indeed, that move toward independence marked the beginning of rivalries, the introduction of rebellion, and the loss of intimacy. From the garden of God's rejected promises, poured a wretched mixture of deception, pride and misplaced desire that esteemed self-rule, opposed unity, and spoiled intimacy. The error has been replayed by "the woman" (that is, all time-creatures) ever since.

Eve became a type of the whole human family because, though she was tempted, she was not alone. *Adam joined her in disobedience*. Eve turned her attention toward the serpent, away from her husband, and away from God. Adam turned his

---

[2] 1 Thessalonians 4:16.

attention away from God and to his wife. There they were, turned away from the headship of their Creator-God, beginning the pattern of self-will that still persists: woman not rightly related to man; man not rightly related to God; soul disconnected from spirit; creation unsubmitted to the Creator. In the Bible narrative, it is at that instant that God addresses the woman and says, "your desire shall be for your husband, and he shall rule over you."[3] God calls Eve to an "about face." She must turn back to her husband. But keep in mind, this is a prophetic call to *all* humankind, both man and woman. *Together* they are "the Bride of Christ." God's call to Eve is the call to each of us, and to all of us: Turn from your independence; turn from your rivalry; turn from your rebellion. Desire your husband. Desire me...

Turned away from divine headship, we live in a breeding ground for faulty ways of relating—rivalry and rebellion, dominance, and passivity. This is quite different from the picture we see in Jesus, who, under divine headship, was neither competitor nor rebel. He dominated no one, and He was anything but passive, yet, as we have discovered, He was in perfect submission.

In a previous chapter, we argued that, outside of God's headship, domination and passiveness masquerade as expressions of submission. Our culture complicates things even further by making them gender specific—dominance tends to be understood as masculine, passivity, feminine. This thinking even influences Christians and their interpretation of biblical references to submission.

Recent portrayals in pop culture of women as powerful protagonists underscore this tendency. Today's audiences cheer when the heroine explodes from the passiveness that the culture has prescribed for her and busts the chops of some arrogant, clueless male Neanderthal. Hard-edged female protagonists compete for supremacy over men with fists and fury on the street, and with Machiavellian wiles in the worlds

---

[3] Genesis 3:16b.

of politics and corporate power. Why the shift toward powerful women? Because there is a reaction against longstanding cultural norms that have equated femininity with passivity, and masculinity with dominance. But the fact is that striving to dominate is not a strictly male activity any more than passiveness is uniquely female.

In the feminine gender-role, dominance may not be kicking and gouging or relentless self-promotion, but seduction, manipulation, and attempts at usurping authority. In all likelihood, that is what Paul was getting at when he instructed Timothy, "let a woman quietly receive instruction with entire submissiveness. But I do not allow a woman to teach or exercise authority over a man, but to remain quiet." [4] The Greek word, *authenteo,* translated here, "exercise authority," is used nowhere else in the New Testament. Its closest English meaning is "to usurp." Other meanings include:

1) One who with his own hands kills another or himself.

2) One who acts on his own authority, autocratic.

3) An absolute master.

4) To govern, to exercise dominion over one.[5]

Paul is not making a plea for passive womanhood. He is warning Timothy that attempts to dominate are not limited to men. In the first century, women were receiving unprecedented and unaccustomed recognition in the church. As they emerged from their nearly servile role, women were easily tempted toward the same notions of power and authority that had corrupted men and lured them from the humble and freely rendered submission that is supposed to characterize the Lord's bondslave.

---

[4] 1 Timothy 2:11-12.
[5] The Online Bible Thayer's Greek Lexicon, 1993. Woodside Bible Fellowship, Ontario Canada.

Passivity also transcends gender boundaries. In men, wounded masculinity can see femininity as safe and succoring. Passive attitudes or expressions of helplessness can sometimes reap dividends for a man who casts himself as a victim. This kind of behavior, though outwardly passive, gains power through manipulation and control. But it is not inherently "female."

Passive behaviors may be seen as "feminine," and dominant qualities seen as "masculine;" they may even be applauded and encouraged as an appropriate expression of Christian gender roles, but they eviscerate true biblical subjection. By contrast, biblical submission is assertive in the will of God and responsive to his commands. It is not inherently a gender thing. It is preeminently a *bride* thing, and that is something men and women must learn together.

Submission as Interdependence

The interdependent union between husband and wife is the clearest image of God that we have. A clue to the intimacy of that relationship is in Genesis 1:27-28: "And God created man *in His own image*, in the image of God He created him; *male and female He created them.* And God blessed them; and God said to them, 'Be fruitful and multiply, and fill the earth...' " (emphasis mine).

There is something in the triune nature of God that is revealed in the "two-become-one" imagery of the bride and bridegroom.

I believe the great significance of this union is the reason that the covenant of marriage suffers constant attack, and the sanctity of sexual union is relentlessly abased in our culture. Why wouldn't they be a target when sexuality and covenant are two illustrations of the essential nature of God, and of His relationship with His creation?

It is often said, as though the statement were beyond discussion, that humans are "sexual beings." I would argue that fundamentally we are *spiritual beings*. Certainly, we have a sexual component, and that is pretty important, but at the core of things, we were made to function spiritually.

At creation God might well have skipped sex and made us something quite different. It was, after all, up to Him. Assuming God is not arbitrary about design, there must have been a reason for giving creation a sexual component. Could it be that His created ones were going to need something that would help them understand God? After all, He is entirely unique. The instant they learned to use the pronoun, "Him" when referring to their Creator, they would know something about God. By assigning a gender to the Creator, there is a point of comparison from which we can deduce God's nature. Adam and Eve (and all human beings) were able to know about God because "He" gave them a point of reference. For example, we know God is like a father and that good fathers protect, care for, and discipline the children they love. God chose to make Himself a father so we can draw similar conclusions about Him. We know God is like a husband, and that husbands are to be bound by covenant to their bride, and that covenant should be unbreakable. God's attitude toward us is like that.

Marriage binds people together in unbreakable union because God's nature is seamless and multifaceted; His covenants are unbreakable. Indeed, because the covenant of marriage is a living image of God, it ought to be held in the highest, most reverent regard. This is why promiscuity or homosexuality are wrong, because God casts Himself in the role of the husband of His creation, which is His *counterpart,* in an eternal covenant. To trivialize or subvert the representation of covenant intimacy between male and female is to defile the image of God that is woven into fabric of creation by the very strands of our DNA.

But here is the place that we Christians crash head on into the old, fallen notions of subjection. Rather than approach subjection as though it were a kingdom skill that we, the bride of Christ, both men and women, need to develop, we have allowed dominance and passiveness to become a rule for defining gender roles and establishing order in the church and home. This promotes a hierarchical view of relationship that is inconsistent with true subjection. Ephesians 5:22-33 is a key passage that illustrates the problem.

> Wives, be subject to your own husbands, as to the Lord. For the husband is the head of the wife, as Christ also is the head of the church, He Himself being the Savior of the body. But as the church is subject to Christ, so also the wives ought to be to their husbands in everything. Husbands, love your wives, just as Christ also loved the church and gave Himself up for her; that He might sanctify her, having cleansed her by the washing of water with the word, that He might present to Himself the church in all her glory, having no spot or wrinkle or any such thing; but that she should be holy and blameless. So husbands ought also to love their own wives as their own bodies. He who loves his own wife loves himself; for no one ever hated his own flesh, but nourishes and cherishes it, just as Christ also does the church, because we are members of His body. For this cause a man shall leave his father and mother, and shall cleave to his wife; and the two shall become one flesh. This mystery is great; but I am speaking with reference to Christ and the church. Nevertheless let each individual among you also love his own wife even as himself; and let the wife see to it that she respect her husband.

If we're not careful, we can hear these words with the ears of a disconnected spirit. That's our natural tendency. Our automatic response can easily default to a hierarchical understanding of what Paul is saying, assigning the husband a dominant role and the wife a passive one. Yet that isn't the example of subjection that Jesus has shown as a child or as a servant, nor in his role as the bridegroom. Those examples hint at a different kind of power.

Mutual Love and Common Purpose

In our home state of Oregon, it matters to many citizens where their power comes from. Northwesterners have a strong environmental consciousness. Spotted owls, industrial pollution, logging, and urban sprawl are all part of our regular media landscape. Disputes about generating electricity cause the most sparks to fly. A local power company decommissioned a nuclear generating facility a few years back, partially because of a grassroots initiative. Now, hydroelectric projects, which provide most of our electricity, are being challenged because they endanger native salmon runs. What Oregonians want is a clean, non-disruptive energy source.

Where does the power come from in marriage and in God's kingdom? From strength and assertive leadership? From unquestioning compliance? God's blueprint specifies a spiritually and environmentally safe power supply: submission to Him. Power and authority were to be released through humility and devotion. In Eden, human beings opted for power based on control and dominance; on the cross, Jesus reminded the world that the true nature of power lies in the laying down of one's life.

If we are going to properly apply Paul's instructions to the Ephesians, we need to remember that the source of true headship is a confident, sacrificial servanthood—the Lord washing the feet of the disciples; bridegroom serving bride. Perhaps this mutual responsibility is what motivated Paul to begin the passage in Ephesians 5 with the often-neglected verse 21, "...and *be subject to one another* in the fear of Christ (italics mine)."

Together, men and women illustrate the nature of God: distinct persons sharing an interdependent nature, a common purpose, and mutual love. They also provide for one another the environment for practicing the humility and devotion that is to characterize a citizen of the kingdom. Marriage is a training camp where men and women develop the skills necessary to *be the bride of Christ.* Notice that women are not exclusively "the bride" merely because they are female, both women *and men* are the bride. The nature of the bride of Christ is not fragmented.

The context for Paul's instructions to the Ephesian husbands and wives (5:22) is found in Ephesians 4:31 to 5:2.

> Let all bitterness and wrath and anger and clamor and slander be put away from you, along with all malice. And be kind to one another, tender-hearted, forgiving each other, just as God in Christ also has forgiven you. Therefore be imitators of God, as beloved children; and walk in love, just as Christ also loved you, and gave Himself up for us, an offering and a sacrifice to God as a fragrant aroma.

Paul's comments at this point are not gender specific, they are to the bride. Christ is the example to women *and* men. Women are to express humble devotion toward their husbands while, paradoxically, husbands are learning to be the bride of Christ. The devotion and humility that Christ demonstrated toward His bride is for a husband to emulate in his relationship with his wife. They mirror one another in their obedience.

No wonder there is confusion and misapplication over the issue of subjection in marriage. When we define subjection in terms of dominance and passiveness, it's easy to fragment the relationship. This happens in two ways. First, the husband can assume that he is to claim the role of the bridegroom and expect his wife take the role of the bride in her relationship to him so he can love his wife as Christ loves the church. As the husband focuses on his role as leader, he winds up being concerned about how well his wife is playing her role as follower. In the process he can neglect his own identity as the bride of Christ in which he is to be humbly devoted to the bride, just as Jesus was. Using Eden as the illustration, the picture is of Eve turned back from disobedience and facing her husband, but Adam is still facing Eve rather than God.

Secondly, both partners can interact as though bride and bridegroom were each a rank in God's order rather than a role. Here, again, is the old pattern of one person asserting dominance over another. This isn't the way of the church. A good balancing passage concerning this is 1 Corinthians 12 where Paul points out that all parts of the body of Christ are of equal importance even though they may occupy quite different roles. Paul exhorts his readers to avoid placing one role above another. His words are as pertinent in marriage as they are in the church more broadly.

This was a radical concept to the first century man. Indeed, it's a radical concept for some *twenty-first* century men! The gospel is nothing if not a radical reordering of earthly notions about power and authority. For the apostle Peter to exhort Christian men to, "grant [your wife] honor as a fellow heir of the grace of life, so that your prayers may not be hindered,"[6] amounted to a leveling of social order. In the first century it was understood that the rights of inheritance were granted to men. Yet Peter calls on Christians to honor their wives as fellow heirs. Relationships in the church were beginning to shift away from "hierarchy." The change can be defined by a simple shift in the spelling of the word. Reverse the 'I' and the 'E' so that "I" follows "HE." That is the order that is supposed to be in creation, every individual subjected, not to other people in some kind of hierarchy, but to the eternal "HE," fellow heirs together. This is not a "hierarchy," where people are empowered by their rank, but an "HEIR-archy" in which people are honored in their *role*.

Of that, there is much to learn.

---

[6] 1 Peter 3:7.

Chapter 11

"Heirarchy"

So how does one go about living in an "heirarchy?" If order in the home and church isn't established by the *rank* of its members but by their *roles* how does the whole thing keep from flying apart in a great power struggle?

Power struggles are only avoided when we apply a different understanding of submission, that views it not as a way of keeping order, but as a way of learning kingdom order as fellow heirs, *willingly subjecting ourselves* rather than depending on a form to impose submission upon us. Willing submission after the manner demonstrated by Jesus is the way we prepare for life in a reconnected creation, a life that is the destiny of those who love Him (1 Corinthians 2:9). The New Testament is the story of the restoration of submission in God's creation. As such, it is the revelation of renewed liberty. Paul put it this way: "the law of the Spirit of life in Christ Jesus that sets us free from the law of sin and death."[1]

Counterfeiter or Banker?

Taking a legalistic approach to the New Testament is the main hindrance to living in "heirarchy." By treating the gospels, Acts, and the letters of the apostles as a rulebook, we risk making submission a mere form. Forms assume that someone, or in the case of organizations, *something*, must play

---

[1] Romans 8:2.

a dominant role in order to establish and maintain order. The results can be troublesome.

A pastor friend told us a story from his denominational tradition that makes a good example:

A group of Christians set out to plant a "New Testament Church." Having searched the scriptures, they attempted to establish a form for worship that they could honestly say honored God's Word. Part of that form required that women were to keep silent in the church as Paul's first letter to Timothy required. Every Sunday the congregation gathered on the front porch of the church building to share fellowship, but as the congregation crossed the threshold into the building, it was understood that the women would be silent.

All went well until the first major snow storm of the winter blew in off the prairie with bone chilling cold. Fellowship was impossible under such conditions, so at a hastily-called elders meeting it was agreed that women could talk in the narthex, but would be expected to restrain themselves as soon as they entered the sanctuary.

Eventually, the elders noticed a rather sophisticated system of signs and gestures developing among the congregation as the wives and their husbands took care of seating the children and themselves. So, at another meeting it was decided that perhaps it would be acceptable for women to talk in the sanctuary as long as they kept it to a minimum and refrained completely as soon as the Scriptures were opened. That went well until...

You get the picture. In an attempt to codify the New Testament, the little congregation had produced a form that was on the way to squeezing the life out of their community. There is a good deal more liberty in the church than that.

Two metaphors may be helpful. First, the banker versus the counterfeiter: Both are intimately acquainted with the appearance of a hundred dollar bill but for very different reasons. The counterfeiter's goal is to make an exact copy of real currency—a counterfeit. The banker wants to be familiar with the real thing in order to distinguish it from the phony. As Christians, we can try to duplicate the first century church by establishing form and dogma, or we can become intimately familiar with the life and choices of the church community as they are described in the Scriptures. The second kind of familiarity makes it possible to exercise Christian liberty. When we are tuned to the principles of godliness described in the New Testament we learn to distinguish honorable church life from something else. The emphasis is not on rules, but discernment. This was the kind of liberty that Paul worked to attain as he encouraged each church to analyze their cultural environment. He wanted Christians to learn discernment so they could decide for themselves which cultural practices they could, in good conscience, accept[2] and which ones violated principles of godliness, or reflected poorly on the gospel. "All things are lawful," said Paul, "but not all things are expedient."

Another metaphor sees the Scriptures as either an anchor or a compass. One observer pointed out that though a schooner anchored in the harbor is a beautiful sight, that's not what a schooner is for. A ship is built for the sea, to be driven by the wind and guided by its compass toward its destination. The New Testament is a description of redeemed and reconnected life being lived, complete with successes and failures. It gives us an unflinching glimpse of both. The apostles' letters are largely refinements and corrections for erring Christian churches. We find our own successes and failures mirrored in the pages. As we navigate the waters of the Christian life the Scriptures become a compass that keeps us bearing down on the work of the kingdom until the Lord returns. The church is

---

[2] 1 Corinthians 11:13. Spiros Zodhiates observes that this verse should be translated, "Decide in regard to it your own selves," suggesting that decisions regarding local customs needed to be evaluated to be certain, "there is no contrary teaching involved." Further, he says, "this whole scripture teaches that existing customs, as long as they are not contrary to morals and scripture, are to be adhered to for the sake of unity and not be flaunted."

not a static institution, it is a living and dynamic body guided by the Spirit through the New Testament scriptures.

Will the Real Bride Please Stand Up?

In marriage, the heir-archical attitude frees men and women from a formula approach and allows them to be partners in the work of submission. Wives are to be in submission to their husbands so he, in turn, can practice being subject to Jesus, his bridegroom. In the fashion of God's original design, the husband must be willing to return his attention to his God, and walk in submission so his wife can turn her gaze back to her husband. When submission is practiced as a form, devoted Christian women often find themselves trying to submit to a man that is trying to be "the head" of his bride without any sense of his own need for learning to be *a bride to the Head*, namely Jesus Christ.

Authority based on the fact that a person is married and male is not *spiritual* authority; it is authority based on position. True spiritual authority flows from the Head of the church through believers who are under His headship, that is, those who are subject to Christ. If the authority in a marriage is merely positional it usually begins to be eroded by rivalry and a lack of respect.

This is why a change in perspective is needed in the church. Submission has been primarily defined hierarchically and practiced positionally. Shifting that trend will require that men and women focus more on the implications of a future life in the Kingdom and less on our structures and organizations. Ironically, when it comes to this subject, women in the church may be the best teachers since wives, by definition, know something about being a bride.

At times, though, I wonder if Christian women haven't shot themselves in the proverbial foot. Since submission is God's power source, then, according to kingdom standards, a submitted woman is more influential in the Spirit than a heavy-handed, rebellious man. A wife, who practices submission to her Creator by choosing to be in submission in her marriage, holds an enormous amount of spiritual influence. Tragically, many women in the church forfeit true spiritual power by reacting against legalistic forms and the abuse of positional authority. Indeed, they often pursue positional authority for themselves, effectively mirroring the culture (see previous chapter). By refusing submission they fall into the state of spiritual anemia that characterizes anyone who chooses rebellion over humility. This is the principle behind the apostle Peter's encouragement to wives of disbelieving husbands:

> In the same way, you wives, be submissive to your own husbands so that even if any {of them} are disobedient to the word, they may be won without a word by the behavior of their wives, as they observe your chaste and respectful behavior.[3]

Here, Peter appeals to wives to take on the stance of a "true bride" that will invite the repentance of a rebellious husband. Spiritual authority based on submission always carries more weight than official authority based on position or a legalistic application of Scripture.

The ideal, of course, is when a husband and a wife both understand submission in their marriage. First, that they are to walk in a working partnership as fellow heirs—an *heirarchy*. Second, that they share a responsibility to reflect the image of God, Christ, and His church through their relationship. Finally, that in their partnership they have the opportunity to learn two other key elements of submission—*humility and devotion*.

Humility and Devotion

God's plan for restoring the order that was lost in the garden requires a community of human beings who have yielded their will in utter submission to their Creator. That is the key to the return of the power of unity that the Creator

---

[3] 1 Peter 3:1-2.

interrupted, by scrambling language in Genesis 11. Such a community will be populated with citizens who bear the qualities of obedient children, and humble servants, citizens who are never more themselves than when fulfilling their purpose in the Creator's restored order. As a servant and a son, Jesus walked in those roles for us, demonstrating the qualities that we are to learn.

The submission of the bride (and, remember, the bride is the whole of redeemed humanity) is found in the relationship between husband and wife, bride and bridegroom. This relationship is modeled differently by the Lord than in the two previous images. Unlike the son and servant, the image of the bride presumes a quality of submission that is vital among restored time-creatures, the quality of *mutual* love.

Certainly, children and parents share a bond of love, but the child doesn't have a lot to say about initiating the relationship. In addition, the parent's responsibility is to pour into the life of the child until he or she develops the skills needed to be self-sufficient. Though our children typically respond to love with love, the dominant flow is from the parent who is chiefly concerned with the needs of the child. This one-way arrangement is why Dr. James Dobson of Focus on the Family characterizes parenting as the long, slow "letting go" of our children.

In his moving little book, *The Giving Tree*, Shel Silverstein uses a tree to illustrate the nature of the parent's role. The story follows the life of a little boy and a tree. In the boy's childhood the tree is a playground, protector and provider. Like most parents, the tree finds joy in that role. Predictably, the boy in the story grows older and more distant, returning only occasionally to the tree for such things that seem important to him: apples to sell for money; branches for building a house; eventually the tree's trunk for a boat. From the first page through the touching conclusion, Silverstein shows that love, especially parental love, can often be more sacrificial than mutual.

The fully-submitted love of God, however, is to be both. Kenneth Wuest, defines this *agape* love in his expanded translation of Christ's conversation with Peter in John 21:15-19. It is...

> a love called out of your heart by my preciousness to you, a devotional love that impels you to sacrifice yourself for me.[4]

> That kind of love applied among believers is to be the mark of the Christian. Indeed, it is the foundational quality of biblical submission.

The parent role doesn't fully address this kind of love and neither does the servant role. A servant, even though he may choose to continue in his master's service, doesn't initiate the arrangement unless forced to it by circumstances. The bridegroom, however, is assumed to share a mutual love with his bride that draws them together in a covenant relationship, and most importantly, *draws out* the giftedness of his bride by his humility and devotion. For this reason, Jesus illustrates the submission of the bride, not by assuming an earthly role, like a son or a servant, but by living out His true nature as the *Bridegroom*. From observing Him as He interacts with those who are His "bride" we are introduced to skills that must be practiced.

Humility and devotion are the qualities that give life to submission. Humility in the biblical sense is not self-deprecation; it is an accurate assessment of one's worth and ability. Furthermore, it is an unwillingness to use those abilities to gain approval or status. Devotion takes submission one step further. It taps the power of humility and causes us to eagerly surrender ourselves to God, to one another, and to the Creator's ultimate purposes.

So far, we have learned valuable lessons about submission from Jesus as He modeled them in the roles of a son and a servant. From His example of sonship, we learned to be

---

[4] Kenneth S. Wuest, *The New Testament, an Expanded Translation* (Grand Rapids: Eerdmans,1961), 267.

obedient and to increase in wisdom, which is to know the Father's mind well enough to act, and initiate action on His behalf. If we seek the character of a bondslave, we train our spiritual nature to practice the willingness to respond and the patience to be available, even when to do so means to set aside our own purposes. These attributes were to be normal for the race of time-creatures. It was at the cross, the Creator offered His creatures the chance to reclaim them. The potential for attacking and demolishing the barriers that resist the Creator's initial purpose is realized as we begin to walk fully submitted to God.

Our submission as children and servants is like an explosive charge set against the boundary between time/space and the stronghold of the rebel elohim. Being in submission as a bride—walking in humility and devotion—is the spark that ignites it. The explosive power of submission enables the Creator's restored time-creatures to advance in unity. Remember His assessment of a race in that condition? He said it could accomplish the seemingly impossible. That being true, a submitted race will succeed in warfare, because it is walking in intimacy and unity with the Creator. Intimacy, unity, and warfare are the subjects of the next three chapters. They are three elusive qualities of spiritual maturity in what we call "the church." Submission is the key to each one.

PART 3

Deployment

Chapter 12

In the Arms of Love

What does it mean that God made human beings in His image? The question has consumed the interest of theologians for centuries. Some cults presume that the "image" of which God spoke is physical: God is an exalted man. On the other hand, Orthodox Christian thinkers have been puzzled about which qualities of the omnipotent, omniscient, and omnipresent God are pale enough to be applied to human beings. Self-awareness, individual uniqueness and self-determination usually wind up among them, but one quality of God's image that is often overlooked is *plurality*. God, though singular in nature is plural in expression. In that way, human beings are like Him.

The Creator Himself made the earliest recorded sociological observation. He noted, "It is not good for man to be alone..." The nature of human beings is that they are created for relationship. Within beings that have self-awareness—personhood—there is the instinctive need for others. The highest expression of that need was man's unbroken relationship with God. Next, was Adam's relationship with his wife. Since then, throughout scripture, God has revealed Himself in terms of the marriage covenant. The intimacy suggested by that choice of metaphor is astonishing when you consider the awesome majesty of the Creator of the universe compared to the weakness of the fallen human race. For some reason in the eternal plan of Almighty God there is a call to intimacy.

Independence and Rivalry

But the condition of our fallen race is one of isolation and estrangement. After the fall, intimacy gave way to independence; independence to rivalry; and rivalry to domination and passiveness. The act of "tree-sin" in the garden was an act of rebellion, a bitter brew of deception, pride and misplaced desire that nourished the condition of self-rule that has been the pattern of humans ever since. Adam and Eve's unsubmitted hearts spawned a competitive, antagonistic race that, without a renewed relationship with the Creator, would be forever locked in a fruitless battle of the wills. Jesus, The Seed, described the doomed enterprise of living outside of relationship with the Creator: "Without Me you can do nothing."

Yet, even having experienced an encounter with Christ, many believers confess to a deep aching for intimacy with God. The cry of many sincere Christians is for a closer walk with Him. In reality, that cry is a mere echo of the heart of God toward us. The words of Jesus as he lamented over Jerusalem capture the yearning that inhabits the heart of the Father: "How often I wanted to gather your children together, the way a hen gathers her chicks under her wings, and you were unwilling." [1]

Dr. Larry Crabb, in his soul-jarring book, *Finding God* says this about the lost quality of intimacy that entreats the human spirit:

> More than ever before, I am convinced that God yearns to be known by us far more than we want to know Him. And His great work in us is to increase our passion for knowing Him until it is stronger than all other passions. Developing that passion in our hearts is a long, difficult process to which God is relentlessly committed. The way is hard, the road less

---

[1] Matthew 23:37 (NASB).

traveled than others, but the journey is worth it. God is immeasurably good and He can be trusted! [2]

The desire in the church for intimacy with God is like a collective homesickness. Recently, our oldest daughter went to Costa Rica for four months. Her husband had been there while in college and wanted to return for additional language study and to relive the adventure of being in a different culture. After three months, they both began to sense a palpable longing to be in familiar and safe surroundings. Though the experience in Costa Rica was positive and memorable, she and her husband found themselves yearning for home. They wanted to see the people in their neighborhood and church community, their house and family. They wanted the warm sense of belonging that was home. Our daughter's e-mail descriptions of what she was feeling became more and more lucid as the time for their return approached. Indeed, we were feeling no less eager for them to be back. There was emptiness in our lives that could only be filled by a homecoming.

The call to restored relationship with God is like that. A need for a holy homecoming is woven into every human heart, yet there is a painful lack of ability to express it, much less achieve it. In *The Naked Church,* Wayne Jacobsen, describes this deficiency:

> We've lost a theology of intimacy, and with it the practical presence of God, which it releases in the believer. This is both the proof and the cause of our nakedness. Having lost the goal of New Testament Christianity, we are adrift in its terminology and practices. In fact, much of church program today is little more than old-covenant experience disguised in new-covenant terminology. [3]

---

[2] Dr. Larry Crabb, *Finding God* (Grand Rapids: Zondervan, 1993), p. 11.

[3] Wayne Jacobsen, *A Passion for God's Presence* (Eugene: Harvest House, 1987), p. 84. (Republished as *The Naked Church).*

Jacobsen diagnoses the problem of many modern Christians: doing over being. Though we live in renewed relationship with God, we act in the familiar patterns of a disconnected life. We trade away faithfulness for success, love for organization, and submission for independence. We gravitate toward order and control, because they are safer than learning discernment or taking a chance on relationship. But,

> ... Submission to God is the key that unlocks God's presence...not just at conversion but also every day thereafter. God's presence will not flourish where it competes with other priorities. He is not our means to fulfill selfish ambitions, nor does he offer his counsel as mere advice to be evaluated.[4]

Put another way, the call to intimacy is like a pregnancy in the church. God's original instruction to his human children was that they should "be fruitful and multiply and fill the earth, and subdue it and rule ..." At the time, Adam and Eve were fully prepared and able to do just that. Though they lived as God's children, they were available as servants. Had they, as bondslaves, acted in obedience they would have been fruitful like a bride. But they broke the line of submission and, instead of ruling over the earth they became subject to it.

Now, as for the last two millennia, the bride has come full circle to God's original command—be fruitful and multiply. The command of the Creator has gone forth again, this time from the mouth of Jesus: "You did not choose Me, but I chose you, and appointed you, that you should go and bear fruit ..."

But will we?

The Way Home

The road back to submission is paved with humility and devotion. I have a friend who lives in a Christian community in Southern California. He defines being devoted as, "surrendering my right to vote" or, put another way, being "devoted." This is a difficult definition for many of us. I, for one,

---

[4] Ibid: p. 87.

like to have my say. Not only that, we like it best when our vote counts in the majority! Learning submission, though, requires a new outlook.

Recently, God challenged my (Jody) practical understanding of what it means to submit myself and be "devoted." Our network of home-based churches has been sponsoring an Alpha Course,[5] which includes sharing (and preparing) a meal for a group of non-Christians, then discussing key aspects of Christianity. During the second week of the ten-week course, I was cleaning up the dishes, when one of the Alpha guests, a socially awkward, rumpled looking woman, came into the kitchen. She announced that she didn't like beans, onions, and meat. Of course, these were the three key ingredients of that night's dinner. From there she listed several other things that were on her list of preferences. Outwardly, I listened politely. Inwardly, I was fuming. Thoughts about choosy beggars and rude, ungrateful boors began to swirl in my head.

In the middle of the night, I awakened thinking about a scripture: Love the Lord thy God...and thy neighbor as thy self. It was a familiar scripture, but this time it had a decidedly different sense to it. "Love your neighbor as *the self.*" The last two words, with the significant substitution of "the" for "thy", were wedged uncomfortably in my mind. I had always understood the passage to be calling me to love others with the same fervency as I loved myself. This time, I heard the words calling me to love others *as though they were me*—a kind of surrogate or replacement self. If the verse had been a mirror, as I stepped up to it, I was to see others there, not the self that I always expected to see.

---

[5] Alpha is a ten-week introduction to the Christian faith that began at Holy Trinity Brompton in the UK. The course is designed to allow non-Christians to interact with the gospel in an open, interactive environment. For more information about Alpha, visit http://alphausa.org or call 1-800-36-ALPHA (1-800-362-5742).

Intimacy with God begins here. The Father has called His children to draw their worth from their relationship with Him, and from that abundance, pour love upon others. Growth in intimacy comes from relationship, through relationship and to relationship. It comes from discovering the will of the Father, walking in obedience, and surrendering our hearts. In other words, growth in intimacy comes from the intentional practice of submission.

In Jewish folklore, there is found the antithesis to obedience and intimacy. According to legend, "Lillith," the mythical first wife of Adam, refused to "lie beneath" her husband. She rejected submission, recoiled from intimacy, refused fruitfulness, and hated—even destroyed—children. She lived in "the places of howling," isolated and utterly malignant in her rebellion. Lillith is the distilled image of unrepentant humanity.

The term that is applied to the race of the redeemed is "the bride of Christ." Here the imagery is borrowed from the intimacy of marriage which assumes a oneness and a sacrificial union; a vulnerable, unguarded relationship with shared goals and unrestrained passion. It reveals the power of intimacy to heal and restore.

The question that faces us is this: will we, the redeemed of the Lord, act as children and obey as servants? Will we abandon our barrenness and, like a fruitful bride, carry to full term a new life that is something other than "self?" Or will we persist in rebellion?

As we discovered in Ephesians, Paul focuses the imagery: a loving, self-denying man and a respectful, submitted woman, living without rivalry and joyfully subjecting themselves to each other. And according to the apostle, Peter, the humble and submitted attitude of a woman—the image of the "true bride"—can be powerful enough to arouse repentance in a stubborn, self-willed husband. Indeed, men may need the example of subjection they see in their wives to learn what it means to be the bride of Christ. Taking the role of the bride requires disclosure, trust, and yieldedness; a restoration of headship and appointed authority. In short, as we practice submission we restore intimacy with God.

The story of redemption is a romance. It is a story of God's unrequited love, His relentless pursuit of His faithless bride. It is the tale of His boundless heart, His passion, His sacrificial quest to restore relationship. God extends to humanity an invitation to once again rest in His love and to be subject to Him as a child, a servant, and a bride:

Return to Me...
Return to your Creator
I have asked nothing save this,
That you love Me.
With your mind your heart, your soul

Love Me!
Return to Me.
Turn from your harlotry.
Turn back...Oh bride of God.[6]

---

[6] Gene Edwards, *The Divine Romance* (Auburn: Christian Books Publishing, 1984) p. 79.

Chapter 13

Key to Unity: All for One

C.S. Lewis' children's stories tell of the imaginary world of Narnia, a land of fantastic creatures and magical beings; yet a land where it is "always winter, but never Christmas" because of the curse of the White Witch. Eventually, Aslan, the great lion (and the Christ figure of the story) comes upon a bleak castle. In the courtyard is a gallery of statues, unfortunate creatures who have been turned to stone by the deceit of the White Witch.

> Everywhere the statues were coming to life. The courtyard looked no longer like a museum; it looked more like a zoo. Creatures were running after Aslan and dancing round him till he was almost hidden in the crowd. Instead of all that deadly white the courtyard was now a blaze of colours; glossy chestnut sides of centaurs, indigo horns of unicorns, dazzling plumage of birds, reddy-brown of foxes, dogs, and satyrs, yellow stockings and crimson hoods of dwarfs.... And instead of the deadly silence the whole place rang with the sound of happy roaring, brayings, yelpings, barkings, squealings, cooings, neighings, stampings, shouts, hurahs, songs and laughter.[1]

Aslan brings the statues to life so they can join him in the final battle against the witch's frozen tyranny. What emerges from the stone is a joyful and wildly diverse army that follows Aslan in an assault on the forces of the enemy of Narnia. Their

---

[1] C.S. Lewis, The Lion the Witch and the Wardrobe.

gratitude instantly fuses with their freedom and unifies them behind their liberator.

It's not hard to see the parallel with the war that is even now being fought over the boundary between the heavenly places and time/space. The race of time-creatures may move about like free creatures, yet spiritually they are frozen and unable to interact with their Creator. In their frozenness they are vulnerable to all kinds of indignities at the hands of their invisible enemy. But the Creator, from the beginning, intended to bring the time-creatures back to life, to enliven again the spiritual component of their being. The Seed of Genesis 3 was the means by which that rebirth was to take place.

The Seed Himself calls that liberation being "Born again." In the end, it comes from being *bound again* to the Creator instead of to the world. This is where the lessons of submission begin. Such liberty, rightly understood, ignites a passion of gratitude that finds its highest expression in submission to the purposes of the Creator. As the skills of submission become normal we begin to experience God in His rightful place in our lives. Exercising submission sharpens our spiritual senses so that we can hear His voice over the interference from our own self interest and from obstinate elohim.

A recent trip to a local 'mega-home improvement stuff' warehouse serves as a good illustration. I had braved the parking lot and gone inside, where I was swept away by a retail deluge. I was submerged in the sounds of loudspeakers, shuffling feet, background music and the constant rumble of the forklifts, their warning signals beep-boop-beeping as they careened along the aisles. Suddenly, I heard the familiar chirping of my cell phone above the racket. In terms of loudness it was no match for a forklift, but because it was *familiar* I had no trouble hearing it. I moved to the quietest place that I could find and answered the phone.

That kind of familiarity with the voice of God is what being submitted to Him is all about. Walking in subjection has the effect of making our hearts familiar with the voice of the Spirit so we can hear it above the many competing voices in our world. Humility and devotion, the key qualities of the bride, give us the grace to bring our lives into harmony—unity—with the heart of God. We practice submission in our relationships with other people so we can learn to hear his voice again, to walk in unity with the Creator.

Able, But Willing?

But, as I have pointed out, our personal character is not automatically inclined to submission, accustomed as it is to disconnected life. By long years of brokenness, it tends to move in the opposite direction. Empowered by the Holy Spirit, we are able enough, but willing? That's another story. It takes practice to do the will of the Master. Practice comes in our daily choices, attitudes and relationships where we learn how to be led by one that is other than ourselves.

Several years ago we advised a young man that was interested in starting his own business. He was a skilled carpenter and felt certain that his abilities qualified him to be a successful contractor, which in fact, they probably did. Upon further investigation, though, we discovered that this young man had been employed by a number of builders, each of whom let him go after a short time. The usual complaint of his employer was that he wasn't cooperative and tended to be independent, even arrogant, in the way he went about his work.

It should come as no surprise that this young man was not doing well in his spiritual life, either. He consistently fell back into destructive old patterns and unhealthy relationships. There was a link between his responses to God and his daily choices. Although he was a talented carpenter he had some changes to make. If his spirit was to learn how to discern the will of the Father, and his soul to learn to be governed by the Spirit, he needed to practice submission in his life. But that's a tough request, especially for guys, because an essential condition for submission is humility and that, for many men (and not a few women), erroneously equates with weakness. But by God's reckoning, humility is the most powerful of qualities. It enables us to wean our soul, the part of us that leans toward self-sufficiency and self-rule, from the world.

As we practice submission toward others, we begin to hear more clearly the voice of God so we can harmonize with Him. Those who walk in unity with Him (like Aslan's army of reclaimed statues) find themselves unified with one another in spite of their differences. Submission is the path to unity with God. Unity with God is the key to unity among His people.

Nowhere has that been more evident than in Pastors' Prayer Summits. These four-day, no agenda, times of prayer by pastors and Christian leaders have done more to unify the body of Christ than any ministry in recent memory. In *Reunitus*, Dr. Joe Aldrich describes unity in action.

> All [of us] would pray—listening to each other and building on the previous petition. Most of us had never met before. It was amazing to see God begin to melt our hearts together as we made the simple commitment to love Him and share our hearts...God was making us one...An Assembly of God minister stood to confess his sin of judgment toward a Conservative Baptist minister. With tears in his eyes he said, "I was told in Bible school that you believed all the wrong things. I thought that you were elitist. Now I see that I was wrong. You love the same Jesus. You believe the same things. Please forgive me."

> The Baptist pastor then blurted out, "I thought the same things about you. But I was wrong. Would you forgive me?"

> The two of them then crossed the room and hugged each other as the tears flowed freely. They didn't just fall from their eyes. All of us in the room were being instructed and forever changed. [2]

The process of unity is sometimes difficult. Years of hierarchy have pierced the body of Christ and left it scarred.

---

[2] Joe Aldrich, *Reunitus,* (Multnomah Books, 1994) p. 15-16.

Healing can only begin if we recognize dominance and passivity as toxic waste products of misdirected subjection, and then beginning with humble devotion to God, learn true submission.

Our carpenter friend is a good example of one who had yet to grasp a fundamental concept of walking in unity with God: being humble enough to allow one's self to be led by an 'other.' He thought because he was competent and self-reliant he would make a good "independent" contractor. Adam and Eve probably thought the same thing. Their unconstrained attitude so shattered their character that God had to fire them from their job as caretakers of the Garden of Eden!

Our 'Sub' Mission

Paul, the apostle, gave the church in Philippi the key to unity:

> If therefore there is any encouragement in Christ, if there is any consolation of love, if there is any fellowship of the Spirit, if any affection and compassion, make my joy complete by being of the same mind, maintaining the same love, united in spirit, intent on one purpose. Do nothing from selfishness or empty conceit, but with humility of mind let each of you regard one another as more important than himself...[3]

The first step toward unity is the recognition that there is one "higher" than we are. We have been so accustomed to operating on the basis of self-will and self-rule that our will strives for preeminence every time we give it a chance to operate. We have thought so highly of our own mind, will, and emotions—we refuse them nothing—that headship, God's rule in our lives, seems intrusive, even demeaning. To continue with that attitude interrupts our fellowship with God just as it

---

[3] Philippians 2:1-4.

did with our first parents. In professing to be wise, we become fools.[4]

If we practice giving God a higher place than ourselves by appropriately submitting ourselves to one another (Ephesians 5) then we learn to be reconciled to God in the process.

In our house, keeping track of the finances is a shared responsibility. My job is to keep the check register; Dan's is to keep the computer records and reconcile the bank statements. Dan's typical pattern is to allow several bank statements to accumulate unopened before he gets around to balancing them. Inevitably, we become aware of a significant discrepancy between the amount that I think we have according to our register and the amount the bank thinks we have. That's when Dan springs into belated action. Sadly, his efforts nearly always require that we lower the estimation of our resources in order to be reconciled.

That is the principle of submission. As we humble ourselves—adjust our value and giftedness downward—we are becoming reconciled to God. As others in our community do the same, we find ourselves not just unified with God, but also unified with one another.

This process of reconciling restores the preeminence of God's mission over our own. It puts our personal goals and mission in second place—they become a "sub-mission." If the lower nature rules the higher one, we lose our ability to function in peace in any kind of society. The result is spiritual, and eventually social, anarchy.

During World War II on Mainland China, Westerners were rounded up by the Japanese invaders and placed in detention for the duration of the war. Thousands of prisoners were randomly assigned to camps where they were given cramped living space to occupy and minimal provisions, which they were told to distribute among themselves as they saw fit. The challenge of forging a community under such strenuous conditions made for an interesting study in human nature.

---

[4] Romans 1:22.

In *Shantung Compound,* Langdon Gilkey describes this micro-society delicately balanced on the edge of anarchy. He observed that domination (by the invasion force) had the effect among the prisoners of compressing the higher values of human nature. As the pressure on living conditions increased, self-centered behavior began to ooze from their midst. Anarchy was avoided to the extent that the prisoners were willing to balance their own needs against the common interest.[5]

In the church, the common interest is the Kingdom of God. To the extent that we subject ourselves to God, we are able to work together. This is the significance of Paul's emphasis on the "body" in 1 Corinthians 12.

> For even as the body is one and yet has many members, and all the members of the body, though they are many, are one body, so also is Christ. For by one Spirit we were all baptized into one body, whether Jews or Greeks, whether slaves or free, and we were all made to drink of one Spirit. For the body is not one member, but many.... But now there are many members, but one body.[6]

The value of self is best understood in the context of submission. Unity is achieved when the diversity, even the disparity, of parts and gifts work in cooperation to reach a goal that is higher than any single person. A key scripture in this regard is John 17. In what is called his "high priestly prayer," Jesus prays, "May they be brought to complete unity to let the world know that you sent me and have loved them even as you have loved me." (NIV) Most often we take this statement to mean that unity is the *goal* and that Jesus is praying that our unity may be perfected. There is another way of looking at the passage, however. If "being brought to unity," that is, "becoming mature" is the goal, then unity becomes the *process*

---

[5] Langdon Gilkey, *Shantung Compound,* San Francisco: HarperCollins. 1966.
[6] Verses 12-14 and 20.

by which maturity is reached. The work of becoming unified requires that we practice subjecting ourselves to others, and to God. By allowing ourselves to be whittled and refined by relationships, especially with those unlike ourselves, we become mature.

Lightning Rods in the Church

One of the reasons that unity suffers among Christians in America is that we tend to preserve hierarchical structure in our churches. Rather than operate according to the principle of "one body with many equally valuable members" we often elevate some gifts above the others. In essence we make celebrities out of those that have "public" gifts such as pastors, administrators, and worship leaders, while people who exercise "lesser" gifts remain non-functional, and sometimes become dysfunctional. The reality is that we have inadvertently created "key roles" that become lightning rods for conflict.

Books have been written about the abuse of power by members of the clergy, and stories told about church members conducting vicious campaigns to remove a pastor with whom they disagreed. Church lore is rife with chronicles of cliques and cadres that gather around "important" figures in local churches. When a key role is vacated, there are usually several wanna-be candidates for the position while lowly servant roles go begging. The problem is that we see the church as a collection of job descriptions, openings that need to be filled, each with its own prestige. What is missing is humility and its sister, unity.

Certainly, such conflicts will always be with us as long as any believers remain who are still "learning subjection," but by "rethinking the wineskin,"[7] and by seeking to remove the infrastructures that foster hierarchy and power roles we can

---

[7] *Rethinking the Wineskin* is the title of a book by author, Frank Viola ©1998 by Present Testimony Ministry.

remove some of the obstacles that make it difficult for Christians to practice submission in a safe environment.

But we struggle to comprehend a church that can operate in mutual submission. That is why we frequently structure our churches like a corporate organization, even though Paul, exhorting the gentile believers, described the church as an *organism*—multiple members functioning cooperatively under a single head who is Christ.

Hierarchy, which is a by-product of dominant/passive thinking, has been presumed to be necessary for effective organization. Over the past several years, though, the church in America has been persistently nudged toward a less institutional and a more relational model of church life. Saturation church planting initiatives, the home fellowship movement, and neighborhood houses of prayer have opened the door to participatory worship, informal organization and plural leadership.[8] The Pastors' Prayer Summits have introduced thousands of pastors to a style of meeting that challenges the common didactic approach that characterizes many churches. Based on the prayer summit experience, some of those pastors have been opening their church meetings to broader participation.[9] These trends, by focusing more on prayer and mutual participation, have called common definitions of "spiritual authority" into question. Without the emphasis on hierarchy, Christians are becoming free to practice submission to one another. In the process they are discovering a new sense of unity.

---

[8] DAWN (Discipling A Whole Nation) recommends the planting of new churches as the best way of completing the great commission. Many of the churches that form from such initiatives are small and tend toward a participatory format with plural leadership.

[9] A challenging exploration of participatory church gatherings is found in *The Open Church* by Jim Rutz (Seedsowers, 1992) and *Houses that Change the World* by Wolfgang Simson (OM Publishing, 1998).

Unity is the state or fact of being one—something complete in itself. The oneness of a complex, organic whole comes from the combination of all its parts for a single purpose. The key to that kind of cooperation is submission—to one another and to God. The result is a powerful unit, for which the impossible becomes possible, a spiritual phalanx that can march undeterred through the lines of spiritual darkness. This is a picture that sends confusion into the ranks of an enemy. It is the power that caused the angelic voices in Revelation 12 to cheer,

> Now the salvation, and the power, and the kingdom of our God and the authority of His Christ have come, for the accuser of our brethren has been thrown down, he who accuses them before our God day and night. And they overcame him because of the blood of the Lamb and because of the word of their testimony, and they did not love their life even when faced with death.

In short, submission is the key to winning the war that started in the heavenly places so long ago.

Chapter 14

The Secret Weapon of Warfare

Put on the full armor of God!

As an exhortation to victorious Christian living, this phrase has ignited many a fiery sermon and served as an inspiration to countless believers seeking a more potent faith. No discussion of spiritual warfare, it seems, is complete without the famous "armor of God" passage from Ephesians 6. Like many biblical phrases, though, it has become one of those "oh, yeah, I know what that means" kind of statements, more symbolic than substantial. Our faith vocabulary is filled with such statements. "Love thy neighbor." "Do unto others..." "Judge not, lest ye be judged." We have become so comfortable with them that they are like elevator music in our daily lives. They may be part of our spiritual heritage, but they play in the background of our daily practice.

Neither do they seem to have much of an effect on our communities. Based on the impact that the church seems to be having on American culture, we have to assume that either the armor of God, with its sword, shield, and breastplate of righteousness, is not particularly efficient in the warfare of the spirit, or there is something lacking in our understanding of its use.

Recent surveys of the Christian population indicate that I am not just being cynical. The progress in the warfare against darkness seems to be touch and go. In the glare of the media spotlight, significant figures in the church world have crashed morally and ethically. Surveys and demographic studies reveal a church population that doesn't differ markedly from the surrounding culture. Divorce rates reflect national norms, rates of domestic violence may be slightly higher, social vices are not atypical, and opinions of professing Christians often don't reflect orthodoxy.

Something is amiss in our understanding of spiritual warfare. Part of the problem is our failure to understand the nature of the spiritual insurgency and its effective use of invisibility and manipulation to undermine the human soul. Part of that successful strategy is a disinformation campaign that has been successful in training us time-creatures toward a habitual misperception of power and authority. We unthinkingly imbue the warfare of the spirit with dominant/passive thinking that poisons our relationships in time/space and neutralizes submission in the dimension of the spirit by passing off a counterfeit of true spiritual might.

Images of Power

Ephesians 6 is a case in point. What makes the passage so attractive to us? Could it be the image of power it invokes? We picture ourselves armed and dangerous, ready to storm into battle and mow down the demonic hordes with a single swipe of our spiritual sword. Without meaning to, we find ourselves seduced by an image of dominating power. We bind and loose; cast out and command; we rail against the powers of darkness and shake our fists in the devil's face. Yet we all too frequently live lives of spiritual desperation.

What is missing in our understanding of Ephesians 6 is context. Hit the rewind button on your Bible for a second. Rewind to verse 9 and Paul's reminder that we have a Master in heaven...back up through verse one: children obey your parents...further back into chapter five: husbands give yourselves up for your wives; wives be subject to their husbands...back to chapter five verse 21 and being subject to one another in reverence of Christ. Go all the way back to Ephesians 5:1 and Paul's exhortation to be "imitators of God, as beloved *children*." Before Paul instructs the church to take up the armor of God, he admonishes them to lay down pride, position and place. The message is clear: power and authority over the evil one depend on learning submission. This formula for spiritual power is repeated throughout Scripture. 1 Peter 5 also contains instructions regarding the fight against evil. "Your adversary, the devil," warns Peter, "prowls about like a roaring lion...resist him..." But prior to this exhortation to steadfastness in the face of conflict, Peter instructs the elders to exercise authority by example rather than by dominating. Further, he tells the young men in the church to subject themselves to their elders. Finally, he requires of everyone humility, warning them that, "God is opposed to the proud, but gives grace to the humble." Wow—to be anything other than humble is to invite *resistance* from God, Himself!

The implication for the church is staggering: If we misapprehend submission we will not only lack power, we will be opposed by God.

Peter learned this painful lesson on the night of Jesus' betrayal. Although Luke's gospel doesn't name him, it isn't hard to imagine Peter as one of the disciples who argued that night about their personal greatness.[1] Earlier, according to Mark's gospel, James and John had aroused indignation among the disciples by trying to get Jesus to grant them ruling positions among them.[2] It doesn't require credulity to envision Peter taking issue with their ambition. Peter was no amateur when it came to delusions of grandeur. It was Peter who blustered that he would never forsake his Lord and who recklessly whacked off a man's ear at the scene of Jesus' arrest. But it was also Peter who abruptly fled in panic and, in a pitiful effort to redeem his courage, crumbled under the insistent questioning of a servant girl.

---

[1] Luke 22:24.
[2] Mark 10:35-45.

After being mauled by circumstances, Peter must have remembered the Lord's remarks about servanthood with new clarity. "The rulers of the gentiles lord it over them," Jesus had said, "But not so with you.... Let him who is the greatest among you become as the youngest, and the leader as the servant." Years after having felt his aspirations collapse under their own weight, Peter's instructions to the elders of the churches in Asia reflect a different attitude in the fiery fisherman. He doesn't command, rather entreats. He comes to them not as a man of position and privilege, but as a "fellow elder." The apostle wrote: "shepherd the flock of God among you...nor yet as lording it over those allotted to your charge, but proving to be examples..."[3] Clearly, the admonition of the Lord found its way into Peter's heart. Peter, then, planted it in the life of the church.

James, "the Lord's brother," identifies the same pattern of successful warfare. As Peter warned the Gentiles, so James warns Jewish believers of God's opposition to the proud, but His extension of grace to the humble. Then, like Peter, he immediately makes the connection between subjection and warfare by saying, "Submit, therefore to God." Then, "Resist the devil and he will flee from you."[4]

That the apostles taught a connection between submission and warfare was apparently the result of their careful observation of the ways of Jesus, Himself. Hints of it are found even in the Lord's Prayer: deliverance from evil comes after affirmation of the Father's will. The seventy disciples of Jesus are sent out on a mission and in the process of doing as they were instructed, demons fled and people were healed. The reason? The disciples were operating as executors of God's will. They were in submission. As a result, Jesus said, "...the spirits are subject to you..." [5]

---

[3] 1 Peter 5:3.
[4] James 4:6-8.
[5] Luke 10.

Let's pause a moment to consider the significance of this scene in Jesus' ministry.

Turning Point

The ministry journeys of the disciples mark the turning point in human history. Not since the garden had the power of connected life been in the hands of human beings. No wonder Jesus rejoiced. He had seen the eviction of Satan from the highest heaven. He knew what the Father's plan was. He knew that once spiritual life had been returned to human beings they would be capable of walking in humble submission to God and return to unity among themselves. As a result, they would be able to exercise the authority that was originally theirs. The victorious mission of Jesus' seventy recruits was an incursion by the army of The Seed. It was the opening shot of the battle in which all believers must fight. Let's revisit Revelation 12, only this time pay closer attention to the nature of our role in combat:

> And there was war in heaven... And the great dragon was thrown down, the serpent of old who is called the devil and Satan, who deceives the whole world; he was thrown down to the earth and his angels were thrown down with him. And I heard a loud voice in heaven, saying, "Now the salvation and the power and the authority of our God and the authority of His Christ have come, for the accuser of our brethren has been thrown down, who accuses them before our God day and night. And *they overcame him because of the blood of the Lamb, and because of the word of their testimony, and they did not love their life even to death.*" [6]

Adam and Eve, in their ignorant self-interest, had become collaborators in a rebellion of eternal dimensions. But this passage describes human beings setting about the task of reclaiming the world that their first parents had squandered into the hands of the elohim. In essence, the first Adam made the mess, the Second Adam, Christ, made Adam's descendants

---

[6] Vs. 9-11. Italics mine.

able and willing to clean it up. When that job is done God's creation will be privileged to see its original purpose, the purpose that faded from view the instant the first humans traded submission for dominion. It is not optional for us to believe that such warfare exists, neither is our participation optional. It is the first task (though not the last) of redeemed humanity: take back planet earth.

The good news is that "the battle is the Lord's." Jesus assured His disciples that "the gates of hell will not prevail"[7] against the church, moreover, the book of Revelation leaves no doubt of the outcome. Still, it seems that we are losing plenty of battles on the way to winning the war.

Paul's first letter to the Corinthians holds some clues as to why. Among the problems that faced the church in Corinth was the belief by some that there was no resurrection of the dead. Apparently, there were some believers there who took the position that "seeing is believing." They hadn't seen a resurrection so they concluded that it just wasn't so. Paul grapples with the issue in chapter 15. And, as he makes a case for the resurrection, he describes the outcome of the warfare of Revelation 12.

> For as in Adam all die, so also in Christ, all shall be made alive. But each in his own order: Christ the first fruits, after that those who are Christ's at His coming, then comes the end, when He delivers up the kingdom to the God and Father, when He has abolished all rule and all authority and power. For He must reign until He has put all His enemies under His feet.... For He has put all things in subjection under His feet.... And when all things are subjected to Him, the Son Himself, also will [make Himself subject] to the One who subjected all things to Him, that God may be all in all.[8]

According to Paul, when the victory is secure, Jesus will have abolished three things: rule, authority, and power.

---

[7] Matthew 16:18.

[8] 1 Corinthians 15:22-28 (NASB).

Christ is the one who rules. Paul uses the term because it implies preeminence and final authority. Christ is to reign for the duration of the war. When the victory is secure He will voluntarily subject Himself to the Father, thus abolishing "rule." The voluntary nature of His submission is important. In the above passage I changed the original "then the Son Himself also will be subjected" to the bracketed phrase "make Himself subject," in order to more clearly reflect the slant of the original language. *The power of the submission principle comes from the willing exercise of it.* The first Adam refused submission. The second Adam, "did not regard equality with God a thing to be grasped, but emptied Himself, taking the form of a bond-servant..." The result of that willing submission was preeminent authority.

Authority is the Greek word, *exousia*. It suggests a delegated permission to act. It carries with it the right to take action on behalf of someone greater. Power (Greek, *dunamis*) is the raw ability to take action. For example, a police SWAT team undoubtedly has the power to break down the door of a house. As deputized officers they may even have the right, but they still need a proper warrant issued by the ruling jurisdiction. They may have the *dunamis* and *exousia* but still lack *arche,* the jurisdiction to take action, the place of rule.

Christ, by His demonstration of willing submission to the Father, even to the point of death on the cross, is the ruling jurisdiction. His work at the cross made power (*dunamis*) available to all who would receive Him, and He, by virtue of His preeminence, delegated to them the authority (*exousia*) to act on His behalf. That includes "the right to become children of God"[9] and the "authority to tread upon serpents and scorpions, and over all the power of the enemy..." [10]

---

[9] John 1:12.
[10] Luke 10:19.

Who's Really in Charge?

Then what's up with the pitiful state of the army of time-creatures these days? If we've got all this power and authority, why do we wind up defeated?

One reason is that we still aren't very good at remembering who's really in charge in the universe. Like Peter, James and John, we habitually get full of ourselves—old habits die hard. Jesus gave us authority and power over demons and the influence of evil, but he never delegated the "rule." He retained the rule so that by our submission to Him we would have unhindered access to the power of a reconnected life. But as we saw earlier, we humans are thoroughly out of the habit of walking in submission to God. If we're not careful to practice the skills of submission, we just revert to "suiting ourselves" or dancing perilously close to equally unworthy authorities just like Adam and Eve did. Such misdirecting of our submission imitates the minions of darkness who were the first to follow that course long ago, sealing their own doom and infecting the human family with the same fatal disease. "Subjected to futility" is the term Paul, in his letter to the Romans uses to describe it.[11] It is the condition of being destitute of wisdom and stumbling off the path to follow a foolish or ill-advised course.

Since Jesus has the "preeminent authority," He, alone is worthy of our allegiance. Victory in matters of warfare depends on using the power and authority that has been delegated to us, but only by the warrant issued by the governing magistrate, that is, Jesus. If we can't make efficient use of power and authority perhaps it is because we have neglected, willfully or carelessly, to be submitted to the source of all rule.

It's a familiar story. People have been trying to act on their own authority since the garden. Remember the story of Ai in

---

[11] Romans 8:20.

the book of Joshua?[12] God's empowerment of Israel as they entered the Promised Land is not unlike our empowerment by the Spirit as we try to get used to walking with a working spirit. The pitfalls they faced shed light on our own challenges in submission.

If you will recall, the people of Israel had entered the Promised Land and, by God's might, conquered Jericho—the "walls came tumblin' down." Their next objective was Ai. In the eyes of "General Joshua" this was no great feat. If they won at Jericho, Ai would be a piece of cake. What he hadn't counted on was the "Achan factor." An Israelite by the name of Achan had decided to take a little plunder for himself at Jericho even though God had made it clear that all such souvenir hunting was strictly forbidden. Achan's lack of submission wasn't discovered until 36 Israelite warriors lost their lives in a thwarted attempt to take Ai. In God's power structure submission is a prerequisite to victory. He said, "Israel has sinned, and they have also transgressed My covenant which I commanded them.... Therefore the sons of Israel cannot stand before their enemies..."[13]

Warfare has a way of exposing the source of our authority. With the "Achan factor" at work, Israel went into battle under their own authority—they tried to function without being in submission to the will of God. Rebellious Achan, rather than obeying and yielding his will to the eternal "Other," had reenacted the disobedience of Adam and Eve. In effect, God had said, "From any of the bounty of the Promised Land you may take freely, but from the plunder of Jericho you shall not take, for in the day that you take from it you shall surely die..." Like Adam and Eve, Achan acted in disobedience and he died; he and others with him.

An incident in the New Testament illustrates the same principal at work. Paul, operating under the authority of Christ had been casting out demons in Ephesus, with some pretty

---

[12] Joshua 7.
[13] Joshua 7:11-12.

impressive results. A group of seven itinerant Jewish exorcists had apparently observed Paul's track record and decided they needed to make some changes in their methodology. Thinking that the secret was in saying the right words, they started "name dropping" as they attempted to route evil spirits. Here is the record of the result:

The incantation they used was this: "I command you by Jesus whom Paul preaches! Come out!" But when they tried it on a man possessed by an evil spirit, the spirit replied, "I know Jesus, and I know Paul, but who are you?" And he leaped on them and attacked them with such violence that they fled from the house naked and badly injured. [14]

Bewildered by my lack of effectiveness, sometimes I have felt like those poor clods! My problem is forgetting that in order to walk in real spiritual authority I need to be skilled at walking in obedience and submission. When we experience spiritual defeat we should consider whether the Achan factor is at work.

At the core of Achan's covetous act and the slapstick blunder of the sons of Sceva is pride. Achan couldn't accept the fact that something mattered beyond his own immediate concern, and the seven brothers wanted results without submission.

To most of us pride is like a possession. We say we have pride in ourselves. We take pride in our children. We are proud to be an American. In fact, pride isn't something we have, but evidence of something we lack.

Let me explain.

Years ago, little leagues across the country started to require batting helmets for the players. Batting helmets are cumbersome affairs, lop-sided plastic headgear with a shield that extends over one side of the player's face. At first, the kids balked at using them because they looked funny. It was a case

---

[14] Acts 19:13 & 15 (NLT).

of youthful, self-conscious pride. But one of the hazards of little league is the cross-eyed kamikaze pitcher. For batters with slow reflexes, getting beaned in the ear proved to be too high a price to pay for a free trip to first base. They humbly agreed to wear the helmets. These days the major leagues require helmets, too, so the kids wear them willingly. Most young players simply prefer the resonant "bonk!" of plastic to the dull "thunk" of the ball against the side of their head. The moral of the story is, in spiritual warfare, as in baseball, it is a good idea to have your head covered. Humility makes a good helmet. Pride may get you to first base, but you will have a corker of a headache...and in a war of the spirit, it will never result in a home run. Pride may sound like a good thing to have, but humility is better.

A Better Way

The danger of pride and the value of humility is well established throughout the Bible. Pride leads us to destruction in Proverbs 16:18; brings us low in Proverbs 29:23; and leads to a day of reckoning in Isaiah 2:12. The point is clear. Pride leaves us uncovered in battle. Humility is necessary if we are to put on the "helmet of salvation." Peter counseled the church to "humble yourselves, therefore, under the mighty hand of God, that He may exalt you at the proper time." We are in a position to be exalted over the evil one to the degree that we abide under the rule of—put on—Christ.

This is why personality driven churches and ecclesiastical power struggles emasculate American Christianity. When we ought to be focusing on the Head of the church, we focus on the church. We become distracted with her structure, irritated and fascinated by her people, preoccupied with her programs, and seduced by her influential places. Sometimes these reefs in our faith culture are hidden beneath a pious "doing it all for the glory of God" attitude, but the numbers game that churches play betrays our tendency to value the world's standard of success. Jesus said that we couldn't serve it and also serve God.

In the New Testament, "mammon" is the term used to describe the allure of worldly power. Mammon—quantity, cost and influence give it its sparkle— hangs above the church like a mobile over a child's crib. More services, better programs, increased attendance, bigger buildings and higher budgets are the baubles that dangle there. If we are careless we will find ourselves fixing our eyes on the things here below instead of practicing the skills of a devoted follower.

Humility and submission work against divisions, factions, strife, and conceit, which divide the church and prevent it from standing. If we intend to be victorious in the battle to reclaim planet Earth, the key will be learning submission. If we don't, we will find God a fearsome opponent. No amount of training in submission—learning the strength of family, the power of servanthood, the ability of a devoted bride—can mitigate the fatal error of pride. The good news is that if we humble ourselves under the mighty hand of the Creator, no weapon formed against us will stand.

Chapter 15

Arise My Beloved

The disaster in Eden darkened the eyes of God's cherished time-creatures. Where there had once been the light of obedience and submission to His eternal designs, there was darkness. The first time-creatures, no longer sensing the will of the Father, turned instead, to one another and to the created world for a sense of order. The curse of estrangement burst upon the garden paradise and became the desolate legacy of every generation to follow. The time-race had been swept away by the currents of a war that had broken out in the heavenly places, a conflict begun by a rebel faction of the eternal race of elohim. It was a rebellion that was hopeless from the beginning, but even hopeless uprisings attract their followers and consume those caught in the zeal of war. The clash that spilled out of the infinite/eternal dimension into time and space, became the genesis of all of the great stories ever told. Stories of heroism and bravery; fantastic tales of unseen worlds and mystical creatures...and love stories. It is the meta-narrative, the repository of legend, and the wellspring of truth.

The Bible is the story of God's project of restoration. It is the wondrous account of His quest to restore sight to the darkened eyes of a rebellious race and bring the time-creatures, once again, into loving submission to Him. If from the beginning, they had learned wisdom and obedience as dutiful children; if they had acceded to be trained as competent and willing servants; if they had chosen to walk in love and intimacy with their Creator, the story of the time-race would have been dramatically different—altogether opposite to a world of anarchy and sin. Such a race would have thought like its Creator. It would have had the mind of God. What was right in the eyes of every time-creature, quite logically, would have been what was right in the eyes of their Father-Creator. They would have been a people who shared God's own heart in submission exactly as He had originally intended. They would have been fellow heirs of the grace of life.

Alas, it was not to be. But the Creator had determined to bring the time-race back, to revive its spirit life by delivering into their native dimension the greatest power in the universe, a power so important that the Creator determined to deliver it personally. He promised to end forever the rebellion in the heavenlies and to utterly destroy its leader by sending The Seed. And so He did. But it was the Creator himself who took on the identity of The Seed. It was He who satisfied the call for justice, and it was He who modeled the life that was the destiny of the fallen time-race, and He who empowered them to drive the rebellion out of time and space.

And it was He, like a Bridegroom calling to His beloved bride, who sought after the errant race.

Three millennia ago, the time of the judges was a clear example of the sin and anarchy that is the inevitable outcome of human society living with an amputated spirit. Two millennia ago a healing began. As C.S. Lewis put it, God had "landed on this enemy-occupied world in human form."[1] At the cross, the veil of separation was shredded as the "Spirit of life in Christ Jesus" burst into the perishing human heart. For twenty centuries that same Spirit has been applying the healing balm of restoration that is *submission,* so that a broken race could "remember from where they had fallen, and repent and do the deeds they did at first..."

Yet, even as the restoration continues, the battle rages. The fallen elohim still wage a war of attrition. They will not—

---

[1] C.S. Lewis, *Mere Christianity*, Macmillan, 1952, p. 56.

cannot—win, but in the fury of defeat a malicious enemy will carry off as many opponents as he can. Someday the war will be ended and you, the victorious warrior, will return from the battlefield...

> to the city of the living God, the heavenly Jerusalem, and to thousands of angels in joyful assembly. You [will] come to the assembly of God's firstborn children, whose names are written in heaven. You [will] come to God himself, who is the judge of all people. And you [will] come to the spirits of the redeemed in heaven who have now been made perfect. You [will] come to Jesus, the one who mediates the new covenant between God and people...[2]

But now is the season of waiting. We wait. The race of loyal eternal ones waits. We wait to experience the fullness of a universe in all its dimensions. The elohim await the discovery of the partnership with the time-creatures that was to have been theirs before the rebellion. Both races wait for the emergence of a new creation, a new heaven and a new earth.

And The Seed, Jesus Christ, the Creator in time and space, waits for His love story to come to its joyous conclusion.

If we could peer into the future we might see what lies ahead.

With a shout of unrestrained joy the eternal Bridegroom—having lived in anticipation of this moment—descends and approaches the dwelling place of His bride. At the door, He speaks. "Open to me, My sister, My darling, My dove, My perfect one!" He extends His hand. She opens to her beloved. She appears as He knew she would, radiant—almost luminous—and eager. Her eyes are clear; her life and body full of light; her heart fully submitted to Him. Her eternal destiny is laid out before her like a fruitful garden. The years of desolation are but a memory.

* * * * *

---

[2] Hebrews 12:22 (NLT).

About the Authors

Dan and Jody Mayhew have been married for 40 years. They have three grown children and five grandchildren. Jody is a special representative for International Renewal Ministries (Prayer Summits) and the founder of Abide Ministries. In both capacities she teaches worldwide about prayer and intimacy with the Father. Together, Dan and Jody minister among a community of home-based churches called The Summit Fellowships and have a teaching ministry. Dan, a former high school teacher, is a minister and writer who writes from a Christian perspective on matters of faith, church and spiritual life. He has also been a humor columnist and publishes his comic work as Dan "Max" Mayhew.

You may contact them at
wings@stonebutterfly.net

Their websites are
http://stonebutterfly.net
http://tween2worlds.us
http://abide.prayersummits.net
http://summithome.org
http://jody.stonebutterfly.net

A study/discussion guide for Sword of Submission is available at
www.stonebutterfly.net